IF YOU REALLY LOVE ME,
THROW ME OFF THE MOUNTAIN

IF YOU REALLY LOVE ME,
THROW ME OFF THE MOUNTAIN

ERIN CLARK

If you really love me, throw me off the mountain © Erin Clark.
Published by EyeCorner Press 2020.
Designed and typeset by Camelia Elias.
Photograph on the cover by Eli Mora, by kind permission.

ISBN: 978-87-92633-55-2
EBOOK ISBN: 978-87-92633-56-9

August 2020, Agger, Denmark

EYECORNERPRESS.COM

For my social media community.
Especially those of you who kept asking me to write a book.

Acknowledgments

Memory is alive. It flows and fluctuates with time and perspective. A book does not. I fixed all my perceptions of the people and events in my life to a page and a time. I did my best to render them fairly and honestly – and with love. I changed a few names where it was appropriate. If you see yourself reflected in these stories, I hope you feel my respect and appreciation.

A few sections have appeared in other forms in literary journals or as Instagram posts and I'm grateful to my readers and editors and publishers along the way.

My deepest gratitude to Mayumi Shimose Poe and Jacob Sheen, Allison Williams, Laura Von Holt, Carolyn Camman, Jessica Lipnack, Brooke Roberts Eikmeier, Sarah Hosseini, Batia Stolar, and Misha Bower whose support and influence on the drafts and iterations of this work from when it was merely an idea to its final shape were essential. If I sent you a piece of writing, and you told me to keep going, you have helped more than you know.

Thank you to Oranjemund, Vilaseca, Algodonales and London, Ontario for being the places that held me as I wrote.

Thank you Camelia for your magic. Publishing with you is one hell of a romantic adventure and has brought my dream to life exactly as I dreamt it.

Thank you Zero Gravity for teaching me to fly and buying my groceries and fixing my wheels and letting me be part of the team – even if my greatest contribution was as a bad influence on your English.

To mom, thank you for letting me tell whatever stories I wanted and needed. I hope you feel freer, too. Thank you also to my brothers.

And finally, thank you to all the disabled writers, philosophers, artists, activists, and educators who came before me and taught me how to take up space in this world.

I have always had the challenge of balancing the desire for everyone to get out of my way with the reality that I need people to get me where I want to go. Thankfully, my life has been full of people who somehow made more sense of that than I ever could and did both: helped me and got out of my way. In every place that I found barriers, I found freedom fighters and liberators and people who encouraged and shared in my adventurous spirit. Many whose names I never even knew. I hope this book will do the same for others as has been done for me: give confidence, permission, space and encouragement and then get out of the way.

CONTENTS

PROLOGUE

Please, Let Me on the Plane
Windhoek, Namibia, January 2019

Twenty minutes before boarding, the gate agent informs me that they won't be letting me on the plane.

I'm in the tiny local airport terminal in Windhoek, Namibia. The plane is headed to Oranjemund, a diamond-mining town on the southern edge of the country.

My bags are stowed on the plane, I'm past security, I'm mid-sip of a latte I bought to access WiFi in the cafe, my eye on my plane's gate.

"Why not?" I ask with mild alarm. Is the flight cancelled and this is my personal announcement?

"Because we cannot assist you," the gate agent says hesitantly, waiting for me to piece it together.

I rush another sip of latte and purse my lips. "I can get myself up the steps," I counter.

"You can't," he insists.

I know the issue is imagination. The airport staff see me, wheelchair, stairs, and throw up their mental hands in defeat. The only solution they can come up with is to not let me board.

I had reached a summit of 2,200 metres in the Himalayas on my hands and knees that year as a birthday adventure. This tiny Namibian plane is not out of my range.

"The commissioner wants to discuss it with you," the agent says, and indicates that I should follow him back through security. My instinct is to stand my ground. But the agent is caught between us with no power in the situation – me insisting on my autonomy, the commissioner on his authority.

As I follow, a familiar fear of a bad outcome squeezes my chest. My phone only works in the café. How will I arrange new accommodations in Windhoek or to catch a bus nine hours through the desert to my destination? My bank card isn't working so I can't even get enough cash to pay for a taxi out of the airport. How helpful will the commissioner and his staff be?

The gate agent holds up his hand to stop me, then disappears into an office where I can hear them discuss me.

"Could someone talk *to* me and not *about* me, please?" I call into the office.

"Hello, my name is Martin. How are you?" says the commissioner. He steps into the hall, towering over me, and invites me into the office.

"Hello Martin, I'm Erin. I'm scared, actually."

"Listen, in situations like this, we don't admit people who can't walk onto the plane," he says gently. "Maybe the elderly, people with canes, but if you need assistance, we can't let you board." He explains that not only do they lack the equipment to get me on the plane but there are also no safety protocols for getting me off the plane in the event of an emergency. He doesn't mention – but I travel frequently so I know – that the only procedure for getting a person with a disability off the plane is to have more than one flight attendant ask the passenger to wait, in the midst of an emergency, until all the other passengers have been evacuated and hope someone remembers to rescue them. I have never had the intention of following that procedure.

Just a small edge of the commissioner's desk is clear of folders and stacked papers. I reach for it and pull myself upright, all my body weight locked into my shoulders and my elbows. I urge the commissioner to stand, to make his arm a stiff railing, which I grab. I push him forward so I have somewhere to step, showing him how I will pull myself up the steps and to my seat without any assistance.

He feels the strength of my grip and the power in my push as I use his more-than-six-foot-tall frame to move my four-foot-eleven, 95-pound body around his office. He is professional, a calm and thoughtful expression on his face despite the absurd intimacy of this demonstration. He agrees to let me board the plane but warns, "The pilot will have to decide in the end. Someone will be with you to carry your things. But you must get on without any help."

I take a second to register that I have convinced him. The tension that had been crawling through my body is immediately relieved. I was willing to crawl across his office floor to show how I could rescue myself, but I didn't expect to change his mind.

My gate agent leads me past the security checkpoint again and out onto the tarmac into the dry blaze of Namibian sun. I sit on the bottom step of the airstairs to pop the wheels off my fixed-frame wheelchair, twist around to reach for the guard rails, and pull my body up, step by step, into the plane. The captain pops his head out of the cockpit to watch. The same muscles that I use as a circus aerialist on the stages of New York get me to my seat.

This isn't the first pilot, conductor, bus driver, or taxi operator who has refused me, but it is the first time I changed a mind.

PART ONE

HOW TO BE A SEX ICON

The risk comes next: little aphid on the pistil, little dust mote in the cosmos, little nucleus caught in the act of dividing. It's the ending that signals Results not typical, Side effects may include... Warning! *Little caveat.*

—RISK: AN ACCOUNTING
BRENDA MILLER AND JULIE MARIE WADE

CHAPTER 1

Better Things to Do
North Bay, Ontario, Canada, early '80s

Starting when I was a toddler up until I was nine, four times a year, my mom and I took a six-hour train ride from North Bay to Toronto to visit a collection of medical specialists at a weekend clinic run for kids with disabilities from all over the province.

We'd stay in a hotel attached to the rehabilitation center. There were elaborate outdoor play villages – entire tiny houses stocked with play kitchens and tiny yards. There were swings for wheelchairs. Inside there were therapy pools; tricycles built for children too big for standard tricycles; and labyrinths made with fabric and imbued with soft light, color, and sound to please and soothe sensitive nervous systems. When I was older, allowed to play out of eyesight, one of the other kids showed me that if you knew the trick, you could make a complete loop around the entire clinic area. Several waiting rooms, hundreds of offices, teaser hallways not to be fooled by. From then on, my favourite game was exploring the halls with other kids. All of us in our wheelchairs and walkers and crutches and bikes, making the loop while we waited to be examined and progressed through our unique levels of development.

There were lots of doctors and therapists being friendly and also poking and stretching and observing every inch of my body. It was like any summer camp – but with invasive medical examinations. There was a lot of walking and crawling around in my underpants so people could watch how my body moved and analyze it.

On one visit, while I was still a toddler, the bowel doctor explained to my mother that due to my neurogenic bowel – the name for the nerve damage that affected the loss of control I have over the muscles in my guts – he recommended I get started on an enema regimen.

I had my own system for pooping. When stool had made its way into my colon, I could press into the fleshy space where my tailbone had never formed and it would slide out. I couldn't voluntarily squeeze the muscles from inside, but I didn't need to. The involuntary muscles worked well enough to get it through my intestines, and my instinctive body hack got it into the toilet. I could feel when I needed to go and I could get it out. But the doctor's concern was that there was a risk that some stool was being left behind. A risk it could cause an obstruction, an infection, do permanent and serious damage, even cause death.

Preventively, and as a general rule in "these cases," enemas were recommended.

The doctor supplied my mother with a series of bags and tubes and instructions, which she gathered in her arms and walked, arms full, down the squeaky clinic hallway. She walked until a memory surfaced from a year or so before, when a friend of hers, another mother of a disabled child, had mentioned that once kids start enemas, they never stop them.

My mom returned to the doctor's office and asked, "When would I stop giving her enemas?"

"You couldn't," he said. "Once she starts, she would be dependent on them."

As my mom tells it, the very first and most clear thought that popped into her head was: "If I do this, she'll never be able to travel."

Not that anyone in our life travelled. It wasn't an option or a dream for anyone we knew. We lived in trailers and government-subsidized housing. My mother's peers had babies as teenagers for the welfare check. They left their babies with my mom to watch while they went off to party and do drugs. My mother didn't take her first real trip until she was in her fifties. The only travelling we did was to these clinic appointments. And yes, I loved it, the clickity-clacking train cars and the hotel rooms and unfamiliar streets. But no one was dreaming of a life of travel. Yet, somehow, travel was her first thought.

My mom cleared her arms of the tubes and the bags, unloading enema paraphernalia on the doctor's desk, saying, "Erin will have to make that decision for herself when she's older. For now, we'll risk a little bit of poop."

Did my mother have an uncanny – nearly mythical – intuition for who I could be and what I could do? Was she clear and fierce, standing up to imposing authorities on my behalf and otherwise getting out of my way in order to best preserve my potential? Or was she a tired, single mother of a disabled child, who was just told she had to add a new responsibility into her routine that I'd be completely dependent on her to perform?

I'd ask that question – which version of my mother should I believe? – over and over again throughout my life. I would swing wildly between feeling like no one supported my freedom more potently than my mother and like no one had ever let me down more profoundly. There was no stable, quotidian, there-for-me inbetween. For a sense of security, I leaned into my innate independent drive; I pushed her out and shut down in almost direct proportion to how much fear and anxiety something caused me. And then I did that to everyone else. I didn't like vulnerability, but I could never get very far from it. I could pretend to be emotionally invulnerable, but my wheelchair would always give me away. I was human. I had weaknesses. Everyone knew it. Instead of learning how to depend on others, I focused on what I could rely on myself for and discounted anything I needed someone else for. But it didn't answer the question I still felt I needed to know the answer to: Had my mother been protecting my autonomy and self-expression, or did she neglect me?

Either way, she had taken a risk. Made a bold choice. Based on her gut – and mine. And it had worked out, by luck or by fate, to my outrageous advantage.

This describes most of my life choices. It describes me. It can be disorienting and tiring, to be exactingly self-determined, but it's also my natural state. It's possible I *have* to live this way in order to thrive.

Because, for a girl with a disability to grow up to be herself in this world, there was no way to play it safe.

When I was thirteen an orthopedic surgeon sliced down the centre of my back and across my ribcage. My spine curved in a C-shape to the right, hunched forward and twisted to the left at my shoulders. I was rapidly growing in every wrong direction, deformed like a tree trunk by the conflict between the force of gravity and its need to face the sun. My organs were liquefying; my spinal column grinding into a paste. The entirety of my physiology was collapsing. My surgeon's goal was to untwist my spine, give me more room to breathe, more room for my organs to function. He used a kind of winch to untwist my spine. He carved a new shape out of my body with saws, shaved my bones down with a file, clamped it all in place with bolts and rods and screws. His scalpel is the reason that, if you trace your finger along the scar down my side, I feel the sensation as a strange tickle in my belly button. He succeeded. The surgery took twelve hours, and the recovery took months, but I could breathe and I was no longer in pain. I hadn't lost as much range of motion in my hips as they'd anticipated because there wasn't enough solid bone left to fuse to. I could bend forward, twist my hips one way and my shoulders in another while sitting down. But the rods meant I couldn't sway, and not swaying meant I couldn't walk. Not freely, not with any ease. I started to use my wheelchair full time instead. For the medical team, the surgery was only successful if I walked through my life. They saw my wheelchair as a failure. They encased me in plastic bracing from my chin to my toes so I couldn't bend forward, which took all my thrust away and made pushing my chair as effortful as walking. They insisted I spend every drop of every kind of energy I had to grant them their triumph.

A neighbour in our co-op was listening to my mom complain about my 'laziness' and figured the problem was one of motivation. Mostly as a joke, he placed a toonie on the sidewalk a few steps away from me and stepped back a couple paces. "I'll keep putting money down, if you keep walking to pick it up." I took his money. But I wasn't lazy. I was suffocating.

I wore the brace for less than a month before summoning the spirit of my mom returning the enema paraphernalia and tossed it into the back of my closet and refused to wear it again.

No matter how much physical therapy I did, walking would never come fluidly or naturally. It would always be a fight to force my body to move this way. Did walking really mean that much to people? Did the measure of the worth of everything they did rest on it happening while on two feet, so that if you wheeled there it didn't count? Or were they making a mistake? When things come to you easily, it's rare that you ask yourself where the value in something truly lies. I was sure, despite their concerns, that walking was not what brought life meaning or created happiness.

It was completely ridiculous to me. It took all my emotional, psychic, mental, and physical energy to make a basic trip to the end of my block. I had nothing left once I got there, so what was the point of being there? I stashed the full-torso brace in the back of my closet, peeled off the plastic smothering my legs, and dropped the whole game. Me against medical authority. Me against society's preferences. The expectation that I would adjust to being corseted got shoved in the closet with the back brace. Shortly after I would stop wearing any leg braces, I would let my whole body – my skin, my mind, my being – I would let myself breathe. I would not spend myself trying to be less disabled – to accomplish someone else's goals, to fit into their literal mould.

I had better things to do.

CHAPTER TWO

A Wheelchair Can't Be a Woman
North Bay and London, Ontario, Canada, most of the 90s

A wheelchair can't be a woman. A person in a wheelchair is often defined by the chair and therefore isn't a woman either. She is an eternal girl-child. Her body can't grow into society's vision of an ideal woman. Forget ideal, she can't even meet the bare minimum societally imposed standards for womanhood.

I experience myself primarily through my senses. I am aroused all the time, frequently by the weather. A breeze on the just-right part of my neck, the slow creep of sun up my thigh as it rises through my bedroom window in the morning. Fabrics against my skin, color palettes in my home, scent of wet nature, thoughts and ideas as they move through my body to get to the page. Music, as physical as touch, gives me goosebumps and leaves me limp. I'll suck my lip into my mouth to taste a piece of prose. The swoop and press of g-force generated by a spiral dive in a paraglider makes my heart as dizzy as a lover might, if a lover could, but I rarely flush erotically over people the way I do over sensations.

Society, meanwhile, experiences me primarily through my wheelchair. Which has no senses at all. It's made of metal.

As a girl, against all the doctors and authority figures in my life, I understood that in choosing the chair, I could not become a woman. I was devastated for the lover this meant I could never have. But the impossibility of being a woman left me free to ask myself what I wanted to be instead.

As a pre-teen, I decided I would grow up to be a European. Europeans had traditions and culture and made delicious food and passed recipes around and knew how to drink wine and talk about ideas and wear clothes and things had *significance*. Europeans were *sophisticated*. I was trying to find a framework for my sensuality before I knew what sensuality was, and it seemed to me that Europeans knew about sensuality in a way my family and community in Canada did not.

❦

My mother started running away from home when she was fourteen. She doesn't remember the reason the first time. But she remembers her mother was more upset that she hadn't left a note than that she had run away. The second time, she left a note. She wanted to smoke, she wanted to cut classes, she thought getting punished at school was enough and that her mother was being unreasonable.

My mom told me once that she thought our lives were so different because I was born with an intuition I didn't get from her. I could *tell* things about people and situations that added a bit of luck to my life. But what if I did get it from her? What if the difference between us wasn't that I was intuitive and she was not but that I had been required to take risks, to make decisions based on what I sensed. It was a muscle I had trained while hers had atrophied. It was normal to want some kind of support, a confirmation of your instincts before taking potentially disruptive action, but my mother had gotten into the habit of letting other people's opinions override her instincts entirely. Sometimes to the point of doing what she *imagined* someone else would tell her to do without even asking, all the while harbouring her own secret sense of things. I grew up seeing her as powerless, watching her circumstances take over her life without a hint of protest. Self-determination is a risk, and what if you're wrong, what if you get hurt, what if you hurt someone else? You can poll the known universe for a consensus on what you should do, but the answer will always be the least disruptive path. I was hungry for choice, I loved the feeling of being incisive, the heavy thud of trust in my urge to explore the world and my sense of myself from the very beginning. And so my intuition, my confidence, my courage, and my freedom all flourished. While my mom had grown up under strict and conservative control: curfews, silence at the dinner table, no boyfriends, no fun. Her only escape from all that restraint was an uncoordinated, mindless rebellion.

My mom ran to friends' houses, to her older sister's, and once to a girls' shelter. She kept returning home every time until she turned eighteen and moved in with my father. According to my mother, though, "That wasn't running away. We got jobs, we were supporting ourselves and living together."

By the time *I* was fourteen, she was a single mother with three kids from three different fathers. Andrew, my middle brother. And Ryan, the youngest. We lived in the accessible unit of a government-subsidized housing co-op. I had lowered kitchen counters, and a mirror in the bathroom tilted downward so I could see myself in it while sitting in my wheelchair. A couple of years later, we moved into a house with staircases and narrow hallways and tiny bathrooms to fulfill my mom's dream of owning her own home. A home – a dream – that did not accommodate me. I hated everything about that house. It wasn't just the physical exertion of going up and down stairs and in and out of my chair to pee or shower or use the computer – by that time the structure of my family had broken down so completely that the only constant was chaos.

My brothers and I had very different backstories unfolding under the same roof, but there was a sense we were in it together – "it" being family, and life – but sometimes what "it" meant was we were all in the mess they were making.

When I was about twelve, we all went back to North Bay and got distributed among our various extended families. Ryan did not have one – his dad had been a short fling, and father and son had never met. I was sent to the trailer in Red Bridge to stay with my dad's sister and her three sons. While we were grating cheese for pizza that night, my father walked in, scraggly beard to his chest, dirty t-shirt, beer gut, trucker hat. The screen door slammed behind him, and he mumbled something to my aunt while I sat there. I watched him for traces of recognition. Something about me that looked liked him; a sign he knew who I was. Nothing. The screen door slammed behind him on his way out and we were still just grating cheese for pizza dinner. I bickered with my cousins. I can't remember a single argument, but I know we had enough of them that my aunt asked me if I wanted to go to the swimming hole with them that day, or if I wanted her to take me back to the city to stay with Liz. It wasn't until writing this that I connected the absent-dad sighting with my cranky mood. I don't think it occurred to my aunt either.

Liz was our babysitter, our surrogate mother. When my mom was unavailable, Liz took me to Toronto for my medical check-ups. We'd stay with her sister, sometimes we brought Ryan with us. She also organized massive Christmas plays with all the kids she babysat for. We memorized scripts, built sets and costumes, made programs for the audience. There was always music and crafting and art when Liz was involved. I remember Liz's affection, guidance, and encouragement. My memory of my mother from the same time is her silhouette in the door coming home from work as the orange sun set behind her, the thick fabric of her matching skirt suits, the tight curl of her permed hair. There was the excitement of seeing her, backlit by the setting sun, and then the memory fades, returns to Liz. Liz making sausage surprise for dinner. Liz singing bedtime hymns whenever I'd ask. She sang gratingly off-key, but the sound was so perfect to me.

During the visit to North Bay, I thought my aunt was saying I was upsetting everyone. I thought she didn't want me. Now, I think it was an honest question about where I'd be happier, but I was so ashamed that I asked to be dropped off at Liz's where I could hide how awful I was. I was watching TV in Liz's living room while she was at work when Andrew crashed up the stairs, his little body shaking with shock. He'd been unruly, as he usually was, and his dad's girlfriend couldn't handle it. They'd packed him in the car and dropped him off outside Liz's house, driving away before he'd made it through the door. No one had asked where he wanted to be. He stood inside the door, crying loudly; his pain was so unguarded, he was so unprotected from it. He was held in place by the gravitational force of his abandonment. How could he bear it? This was why he destroyed everything. I wanted to destroy everything with him. I vibrated with his torment like a plucked harp string. It was just me and Andrew in Liz's overstuffed apartment in a harmony of so much pain we could hardly breathe. Did I explain why he was there when Liz got home? Or did he have to find his own words for being unwanted by his father? I don't remember moving from our positions. We shivered by Liz's front door, together but not touching. Liz knew how to handle Andrew, but being handled and comforted are not the same. His memories of her aren't fond like mine. He still remembers that one time she made him take a timeout by kneeling on a broom handle facing a door for so long, he could barely stand up after. Did she comfort me? I wouldn't have admitted I was hurt by my experience. I would not have known. Shame always hit me first. Then barricades of silence. And I can't ask her. Liz is dead. There is a lot of death coming in this memoir, most of it suddenly.

Andrew always ruined everything. He snuck out one morning to unwrap all the presents before Christmas morning. He knocked over the set of our pageant play during one of our performances. I vividly remember Liz dragging him by the ear from the swamp at one end of the housing co-operative to our home at the other end. He was completely naked and caked in mud, his clothes lost to the bog. In retaliation for being grounded, he spent that afternoon tossing things from his bedroom window into the neighbour's yard. All these events seem funny to me now. I don't mean the memories, those are loaded with distress. I mean, if one my friends were to text they had just dragged their naked and muddy child out of a bog across the neighbourhood for everyone to see, I think we'd both be killing ourselves laughing. But I suspect this is partly a trick of memory. I can recall the most absurd moments, and they end up carrying a daily accumulation of dread and tension I can longer fathom.

Nothing was sacred to Andrew, except for maybe Nintendo and *Star Trek*. I learned to hide what was precious to me. Not just physical things he could destroy but also games and reveries his behaviour could interrupt and erase. I also hid what hurt me. When Andrew's suffering showed pure and blazing, it was like he was a conduit for all the pain in our family unit. Whatever we could not express – or let ourselves feel – found its way to ground through him, tearing him apart in the process.

We moved to London, Ontario, when I was nine. We left Liz, my mom left her job. She expected there to be more support, more services. London was a bigger city and her family – her mother – was there. I didn't have to travel to Toronto for doctor's appointments because London had a medical centre for disabled children. But without Liz, without the respite services provided by local charities in North Bay, there was nothing to support her, as Andrew became more violent. Her mother, my grandmother, was generous with useless advice and judgements. My mother received welfare for a while, and my image of her shifts from her coming home from work to her going "on strike" in the middle of violence and destruction. She would retreat to her room, close the door, turn off the lights and leave us to it.

I was naturally self-regulating, I would have made a great only child to her hands off parenting. But Andrew needed structure, and Mom's rules were arbitrary and desperate and easily broken – she didn't have the energy to enforce them. If she was in a good mood, certain things were acceptable. If she was in a bad mood, certain things could be punished. None of us had any clear idea of what was good or bad. I tested the range of what made a good person quietly and socially. Andrew tested it out behaviourally and raucously. I had the energy, the focus, and the innate stability to keep things under control, but I also had no authority and no way to mete out consequences. I attempted reason, I attempted intimidation, and then I eventually did the same thing you do in a bomb shelter: hunker down, listen to your world end, and prepare yourself to assess and accept the inevitable damage. Ryan, the baby, bore the brunt of Andrew's unsupervised outbursts, and later began to imitate him until he actually outstripped him in his capacity for misbehaviour. Both were raised more by reprimand than affection.

I know now that my mom had frequent migraines, and her retreats from the chaos of us weren't necessarily in the *middle* of dangerous moments, or for very long. But it felt dangerous all the time. We verged on danger constantly. Danger occurred unpredictably. My mom memorably retreated. My memory linked the two: Danger. Absence. It linked vignettes of sibling fights and Mom's closed door.

Andrew refused to go to school for four months while he was in grade six. My mom home schooled him until the school board told her that she could continue to do that, but the school would not be able to provide the textbooks and learning materials she was using – she would have to officially become his teacher and develop his curriculum. She forced him back to school. The first day back he took a reading placement test that showed his comprehension at the same level as a professional journalist. Maybe his unspent intellectual energy was the cause of his unrest. He was bumped up to grade seven, but within days his behaviour was so out of control that the special education teacher assigned to him packed him and my mom in the car and drove them to Children's Aid. There they placed him in a children's psychiatric facility to assess where to place him long term. He never returned home.

Ryan spent a year running away every day on his way home from school. He would usually wander home late into the evening, but he was only nine, and legally the police had to be called every time. "We filed 237 missing person reports on him," my mom said. Once when he was about twelve he didn't come home for an entire weekend. He eventually told the police that they could keep bringing him home and he would keep running away until he got what he wanted. What did he want? To also be placed in Children's Aid. He bounced from family to family and group home to group home. He also did not return home.

Everything – even all the normal things that should have been mundane and boring – everything, every day for nearly 15 years was high-alert levels of serious and dangerous. It was even scarier to feel how disconnected from it all I could be. I never cried or felt upset the way you 'should' when someone you love is missing. I was numb. I would imagine the police telling us they had found Ryan's body, to see if I could summon feelings. The trouble with that was, if it worked, I felt fake. If it didn't work, I felt dead. My feelings had been wrung out and manipulated so consistently for so long, they only worked in fantasies. I could feel things that I imagined. I couldn't connect at all to real life.

I was fourteen and then sixteen when my brothers' lives diverged from mine. They lived in foster care, group homes, a rehabilitation facility, the streets. I lived at home, with friends, in foreign countries.

Those moments, when my brothers did not come home again and I was relieved each time, may have been where I got my ideas of what made a loyal person, and that I wasn't one of them. I would skim the tops of relationships so I could never fail anyone the way we had failed my brothers. They were the moments when my fetish for devotion was formed.

I had no family, no bond that hadn't succumbed in some way to dissolution. I didn't have examples of what loyalty and devotion were, or how one practised them, so I crafted from the shadows. I would teach myself the contours of devotion from what I knew for sure it wasn't. From its silhouette.

"Do you think I would have participated in the family tradition of running away if I physically could have?" I asked my mom, trying to imagine me arriving at a shelter for girls or living on the streets as my brothers had.

I was well aware of how little of the world was accessible to me. I was attending a high school that was accessible only through the use of the janitorial freight elevator. I had already learned that the world was not eager to help me figure it out if I showed up in places I was not expected. And I was not expected anywhere. I was not safe at home, and there was nowhere for me to go.

My mom pondered my question. "I don't think so, you had your books. Travelling was your ticket out. Final freedom."

Before final freedom, when I was 16, I spent every weekend at my friend's house for an entire year, pretending in my mind that I was actually a part of their family. We would watch episodes of *South Park* with her sister, and sneak downstairs to the computer in her dining room, shove pillows around the CPU so the noise of the internet connection wouldn't wake up her parents, and chat on ICQ.

Maria's mother would make home-cooked Polish food every dinner. Her father was studying poetry and writing a thesis on *The Flowers of Evil* by Baudelaire. They had bookshelves full of philosophy and poetry. Maria had a framed print of Picasso's *Man of La Mancha* above her bed. They had a wild sparrow as a pet.

Our friendship ended abruptly when her mother got pregnant. I remember the phone call when she told me, how devastated she was that the family – which had such a perfect dynamic with the four of them – would now be ruined by a baby. I didn't entirely understand the problem and shrugged off her tears. I think my coldness pushed her away, but we never talked about it. I moved across town shortly after and we lost touch. Looking back, I think I get why she was upset. Her home was my sanctuary, but it wasn't my reality. She felt her safe and known foundation being threatened, maybe for the first time. The fact that mine was under constant threat didn't make it easier for me to empathize with her grief, it made it harder. Grief was my resting state. I couldn't even identify it, let alone be comforting and sympathetic while my friend expressed it.

"I think, even back then, you didn't want to make things harder on me," my mom said, answering my question about me being a runaway.

I did run away, but only an afternoon at a time, to the kitchens and libraries of neighbours and friends. I learned to prepare the smoothest quiche, tomato soup from scratch, the right texture of risotto. I had family dinners with other people's families who discussed books and world events with each other. When I was fifteen, a camp counsellor had our cabin of disabled girls row our canoes out into the middle of the lake, where she read a story from *Women Who Run With the Wolves*. I lay down in the bottom of my canoe and watched a swaying twilight and felt myself *change*. I asked to borrow her book and read it by flashlight inside my sleeping bag all night. I understood nothing of the allegories, of the wild soul of a woman, of my own soul. But I desired more knowledge. I asked quirky, intellectual adults for lists of more books like that. I had conversations with them that were way out of my league. They admired my mind, and I preened. I taught myself to appreciate wine and poetry. I acquired a taste for espresso. I developed *preferences*. I promised myself I would learn foreign languages. I would wear lingerie. I would be a passionate lover, if the time came to love. I would have soul.

CHAPTER THREE

True Adventures
London, Ontario, Canada, early '90s

When I was fourteen, my favourite book was *The True Adventures of Charlotte Doyle.* A thirteen-year-old girl, the only passenger and female on board the *Seahawk,* ends up in the middle of a mutiny. In the end, her father reads the journal in which Charlotte recorded the events of her voyage and accuses her of lying and throws her journal into the fire. She defiantly writes the entire story down again in the margins of the books he forces her to read as punishment. Then, in the wane of night, she slips off the finery of her father's riches, puts her sailor's clothes back on, and rejoins her ship.

I wanted that story for my own life. The villainy, the loyalty, the intensity, the bravery, the self-sufficiency, the adventure. Charlotte faced the ways her being was shaped and determined by her upbringing, paternal influences, all those expectations during the 1800s of what an affluent young lady should be. She upheld them sincerely and innocently, then disavowed them when they proved unjust. She determined herself.

One of the characters says at one point: "A sailor chooses the wind that takes the ship from safe port... but winds have a mind of their own." Which is a thing about self-determination and freedom that is often overlooked. It's only the choice to start that is up to you. The rest... unfurls.

I would get to live my life by the wind, going where I could and where I wanted – by fight and by fate. There would be less mutiny and murder, but I would have my Charlotte Doyle dream. But before I knew that was possible – because I could not yet bear to admit it was something I desired – I lied. About everything.

I told people that I had grown up hopping between European countries, living with different sets of grandparents and extended family until I was nine and came to Canada to live with my mother. I pored over atlases and memorized cities in countries I was drawn to; I borrowed details from things I read or from other people's stories of their lives and experiences in Europe. I don't remember what reason I invented for why my mom had left me or why she was in Canada. I felt estranged from my family even though they were around me all the time. I felt alone, like an outsider everywhere. The story of a childhood roaming Europe made the inexplicable seem sensible. Of course I didn't feel strong family bonds – I hadn't really grown up with them. And of course I was an outsider, I wasn't really from here. And it was okay that I felt alone – I was made for adventures. If I hadn't come from this place, I could leave it. I felt so aligned with my stories, the relief from my everyday life they brought me drowned out any anxiety caused by living inside a lie. And I was sure I was pulling it off – that my weaving of my desires, other people's anecdotes, and encyclopedia facts was masterful, subtle, just the right touch.

"You used to lie so much in high school, I forget I can ask you questions now," a friend said to me when we reconnected years after graduation. We were sitting at a picnic bench in a park in our hometown, the breeze lifting the leaves back and forth to let the light flutter across the wood slats.

"What do you mean?" I asked.

"If I asked too many questions, it would get awkward. So I just stopped questioning you about things," she said. Her lack of reproach stuck me as generous.

"Why did you bother being my friend?" I asked.

"I liked you," she said. Knowing she didn't have to be careful to avoid catching me in a lie meant she got to be more honest in return. We could both relax.

I had stopped fabricating entire lifetimes, because the urge to do it had been purged in the process of understanding why I was doing it in the first place. I didn't need to lie if what I was lying about could be true. The lie version of a wild and full life was safer than the desire for the true version. I could experience it all happening right now as I spun the story, and I didn't have to risk disappointment or failure. Society was very clear that a disabled life was worse than death, because devastating disappointment was inevitable. I was lying because I was afraid to want what I really wanted. Life itself.

When I was nineteen, the opportunity to go to Kenya as a volunteer came up. The suffocation of my home life was so acute, that to me it was an obvious choice. Other people were nervous and skeptical and shocked, but I felt calm and certain. Being alone on the other side of the world was better than where I was.

Being alone on the other side of the world taught me that I could make impossible things happen, I could satisfy my deepest desires. Once I knew that, the urge to lie died. I had a new urge. Live more of that life. When I dreamed of something, when I felt it in me, my imagination had a job to do: create the most fantastic visions of life and keep them vivid while I found ways to make them real. It would take me much longer to realize that I had been unconsciously coping as a child and teenager using the same skills and impulses I now use as a writer. Before I even knew what it was or how to harness it, my art had been with me, protecting and guiding me. Showing me how to dream myself into existence.

The first time I felt the intimacy I could share through writing, I was in grade twelve. I had made a swift connection with a girl named Misha, who carried around a massive dictionary to look up words in books she was reading. She wrote plays with wry dialogue and subtle metaphors and had shaved her red hair to a tight buzz, which made everyone think she was a lesbian.

I had confusing feelings for a friend who was making himself a doctor. Confusing because I felt no sexual urge for him like I thought I should, considering I was otherwise madly infatuated with him. If I didn't want to have sex with him, didn't that mean I didn't want to date him? So what did it mean that I had extravagant romantic fantasies about him? What did I want?

I wanted to go to Ottawa. He had gone to Ottawa that summer, and it ignited my lust for travel and yearning for adventure. As it turned out, Misha also wanted to go to Ottawa.

We looked up train schedules on the library computer and (most astonishingly, considering our age and lack of travel experience) followed through on our spontaneous plan. We booked a shared room at Verbena's B&B and, barely knowing each other, off we went.

Each day we wandered around the capital city of Canada in the humid and sparkling heat. We'd walk home holding hands so Misha could jog, pulling me along, and I'd roll effortlessly next to her and enjoy the speed.

Lying in our single beds, separated by a nightstand, we wrote about the things we'd seen. The ByWard market, the National Gallery, parks and malls and parliament buildings and monuments, strange buskers with dulcimers, and new moods I'd never been in before. Then, before going to sleep, we read aloud to each other what we had just written. Misha purred and sighed over my descriptions of the day – despite the fact that she had been there firsthand to experience them.

Then I had confusing feelings for Misha, too. Who was not a lesbian. But what was I?

A writer. That, at least, for sure.

I was most myself on the page. When I was being read, whatever I was doing, seeing, feeling, and how it was shaping me was being witnessed. By people I cared about. By people I didn't even know. I existed. I was creating myself and being created as people watched. *Because* they watched.

I had been watched my whole life. Leaving my house meant being observed. Approached, interrupted, discussed. But that was all through the lens the public had for disabled people. They thought they knew me because they saw my wheelchair. When I wrote, people saw me through my own lens. A lens I could adjust until I got the image just right.

I aged out of high school, I did not graduate. The year I was eighteen, when I should have been doing homework and attending class, I stayed in bed almost every day. I lived in the granny flat above my mom's house. I had my own kitchen and bathroom, living room and two bedrooms. I decorated, I cooked meals, I had friends over and we sat on the roof of the addition at the back of the house on quilted blankets and drank tea and wrote poetry. There were beautiful moments in my life, but I was drowning. I claimed mysterious illnesses, and being disabled, no one, not even my mom, argued with me. This was the course expected of me. To waste away.

I dreamed all day long. I would torture myself with devastating romantic fantasies. Someone usually died. Sometimes it was me, sometimes it was my fantasy love. I had been obsessed with Lurlene McDaniel's books when I was younger. Teenagers fall in love and then one of them gets a terminal illness and dies. The grief in those pages was raw and gorgeous. The love was pure and all-encompassing and could never be ruined. My imagination was trying to find a way to meet my terribly desperate need to be loved while acknowledging my total certainty that it was impossible. Death was not a rejection. I would be filled with sorrow for all of my life, but I would know I had been loved.

It wasn't the only content of my fantasies. I also imagined my success, my adventures. I was interesting, sexy, independent – that's why I was loved, an essential part of the fantasy. But always something happened to take the fantasy lover away from me by no fault of his own. My mind could not sustain a fantasy in which I was just loved. When I tried, instead of a beautiful landscape of the purest grief, I was plunged into something chilling and nauseating. There was something in me, a dark and shameful force that didn't deserve to be loved. If I pushed into it too far, I would drown in it. If someone loved me and then stayed in my life, they would inevitably find out that I was empty, dead, the kind of girl who didn't care if her brother died, fundamentally undeserving. To protect myself from that happening, I told myself that love and romance was pathetic – it made me pathetic to care about it. Which was proven by the fact that I was failing high school to lie in bed all day and dream myself into emotional oblivion.

I wonder if a person can use emotions like some people use drugs. Was I binging on sadness and unworthiness because it felt like a release? I could cry until my throat was dry and my sinuses ached over imaginary people in made up circumstances in a way I could not and never did cry over my real life. It was like I had tucked my feelings away so they couldn't hurt me, only to discover that without them I couldn't get through a day of classes and socializing and being around my family, but I could only be with them when I was alone and in my imagination.

CHAPTER FOUR

Father Figure
London, Ontario, Canada, 1997-2008

When I was in grade four, our class had a pottery lesson. We got into pairs and made rectangular boxes out of clay. My partner was a boy named Seamus. Our box was perfectly measured, the seams smoothly glued by our wet fingertips. We even had a lid. I remember his name because when our box was ready to be sent to the kiln we sat on the bench outside the classroom, under the coat rack nestled in the down-filled jackets and decided what to write on the bottom.

"Do you want to write 'Seamus and Erin'?" he asked. "But with a plus sign?"

"Oh, you mean with a heart?" I asked. And he did. He meant with a heart.

"We could put a heart next to it... or put our names inside the heart... if you want," he said. I wish I could remember how he looked when he said it.

We signed our clay box: Seamus + Erin. Inside a heart.

Seamus wasn't the last boy who would be sweet on me. Sweet with me. But he is one of the last ones I would be sweet to in return.

Before puberty, a disabled child is a pure, sexless angel of soul perfection. After puberty, society still wants us to be pure, sexless angels of soul perfection, but we are not sexless. Hormones come for us, too. Desire changes us, too. Desire to be wanted, to be touched, to be loved.

While our peers date and crush and freak out and figure their sexual needs and feelings out, disabled people are told – perpetually – that part of growing up isn't for us. Sex with us is a taboo, romance with us is embarrassing. No one will love us that way.

Some people are trying to prepare us. Some are genuinely trying to sympathize. Some are still thinking of us as pure, sexless angel babies who couldn't possibly care about dumb romance one way or the other. None of them realize they are creating the reality for us as they speak.

Teenagers, ravaged by hormones, are not the most equipped to deal with the social and emotional complexities involved in dating in general, let alone dating as disabled. It was not like I could calmly talk a cute boy through it – I was *also* losing my mind with sex fever and hormonally induced identity crisis. But I did know this: if he hadn't figured out that he wasn't supposed to like me that way, someone would point it out to him soon. There were still boys who were sweet on me. Sweet to me. But I had gone cold, a bit mean.

The next boy who was sweet with me lived in the co-op housing complex next to mine. We were in grade six and hung out all the time. He knew what catheters were because his dad was a medical supplier. I tried to hide mine once and he told me he didn't think it was weird that I used them.

One summer, he went on vacation and brought me back a comb. The comb was teal plastic with thick teeth and it had ERIN printed on it in pink letters. He knocked on my door, his dark eyes and very sweet face happy to see me, and delivered me a gift. It stung. Like a thousand wasps swarming my sternum. Why did a romantic gesture, a visibly open heart, his total acceptance make me feel pain?

The next thing I remember, we were in the playground of his complex. I had climbed up to the top of the slide or the monkey bars and he was on the ground asking if I wanted to play. I mocked him for asking. I was punishing him for *wanting* to play with me. I taunted him for exposing his feelings so blatantly, I was mad that he clearly felt the wrong way. It was *wrong* to like me, and he should know.

I kept the comb for a long time. We were in grade seven and eight together, but we weren't friends anymore. I was more comfortable being friends with people who were a little mean, people more like me.

My mom married when I was sixteen.

Tony used to drive me around London to show me how to spot a crack house. I don't remember anything he said, just the time spent driving around with him while he told me to watch out. These were not things he would tell my mother; he protected her from the harsh world he knew. But he shared it with me. He wanted to pass on his knowledge to me, and the knowledge he had, he learned on the streets, dealing and doing drugs and still being alive.

Ryan ran away in the middle of a rainstorm one night that year. He was twelve, so we had to call the police after a few hours. Ryan walked from one end of the city to the other, calling home from a payphone while our living room was full of police officers. While a cop kept Ryan on the phone trying to coax a location out of him, Ryan teased him by refusing to come home or disclose where he was. By now, I felt onto this game – the point of it was to upset us. To cause a disruption and then to taunt us for being disrupted by it. I was free to concede the fight, I could choose not to care whether he came back or not and refuse to be manipulated. My mom was not so free. Nor were the police. And instead of supporting my mom through this gauntlet of psychological and emotional fatigue, Tony came home drunk and passed out downstairs while my mom gave another police statement trying to explain Ryan's behaviour and the hopelessness of the situation.

The next day, I sat the family down and told Tony, "You are now part of this family. You have an obligation to be the best person you can be. That's what you told me you were going to do when you married Mom, and that's not what you did last night. She needed you and were not here for her." He hadn't been there for me, either.

I don't remember this at all. My mom has to tell me, quoting my words back to me. "You let him *have* it, and it was *brilliant*." It makes me uncomfortable to hear it as an adult, not proud. But I can't place exactly why I don't mentally fist bump the balls on my teenage self.

Tony was apparently quiet while I talked, but later he accused my mom of not standing up for him, that it had been unfair that I was picking on him.

"I told him you had every right to say what you did," my mom tells me now. "I wish *I* had said it. And it *worked*."

Tony didn't have another drink for several years after that.

When I was organizing my trip to Kenya, Tony gave me money to cover the expenses fundraising didn't cover. He showed his affection with gifts and money and opportunities to make money and connections. He once picked up extra scrap metal at whatever demolition site he was working to save up a chunk of money. He took me on a shopping spree to buy clothes from the "fancy" store I adored at the time. I felt cool in the outfits, especially the boat-neck shirt I wore for years: grey, with a three-quarters sleeve and three white stripes across the chest from Club Monaco. But my favourite expression of his love was the gift of time. He spent a lot of time with me.

It was Tony who took me to the bus station on the day of my flight. He followed the bus as far down the street as he could to stay in my view, waving with his whole body.

But by the time I got back from Kenya, Tony was using drugs again. He had started renovations, but had stalled leaving massive holes in the walls, exposing the veins and arteries of water pipes and electrical wires. Scrap metal piled up in the unkempt yard and on the front porch. Our house looked like the places he had taught me to avoid.

My mother retreated from the world like she had when I was young. I recognized her signs of depression instinctively, though not consciously. After Kenya I moved to Ottawa with a friend. When I would leave again after short visits, my mom stood at the door and waved goodbye to me through the window. I'd look back and have the distinct impression she was waving at me from inside a prison made by Tony's moods. I wanted, desperately, to save her.

She never said he hurt her, but there are other kinds of violence than physical, and I could see the evidence of it in the house and her sense of helplessness. I could feel it in the air.

I went to Kenya a second time, and I was back in London on a brief visit, soft-footing in my family dynamic while Tony did what he wanted, on his schedule, demanding that we accommodate him and sleeping off his benders on the living room couch.

Ryan came over one afternoon. I didn't see what happened, but I did hear Tony shouting "faggot" and watched as he pulled my brother out of the bathroom by his ear and tossed him out the door. I grabbed the corded phone in the front hall and went to the door to watch.

Chaos doesn't startle you after a while. Disaster is not something to escape but rather something you anticipate and prepare to cope with. You let it shape you in order to survive it – and the disaster Tony was wreaking was shaping my mom.

I had been out of the house for so long, and so far away, I had developed an uncanny instinct for freedom. Tony's outburst at Ryan was a threshold that could be crossed. I could see a way out for my mom.

Tony released Ryan on the sidewalk and stormed back inside to see me, sitting with the phone in my hand.

"What the fuck were *you* going to do?" he yelled.

"Call the police," I said.

He pulled the phone out of the wall, tossed it in my lap, and kicked the frame of my chair to push me back. "Then fucking call them," he spat.

I went into my room and sat against the door and called my mom at work from my Nokia flip phone.

"Tony is drunk, he just kicked Ryan out, he just kicked my chair, and now he's stomping around and shouting and banging on the door. If I call the police, they will take him away. Is that what you want, mom? Do you want him out?"

She breathed out. "Call them."

I knew what I was doing. I had learned that when things got out of hand, you called the police to restore order. To protect my brother and my mom, I would have to betray Tony, the only father I knew. Who loved me and loved my mom and had protected and cared for us in his way. But that love had been ravaged by addiction, his bigotry against my brother, and their impenetrable dislike for each other, and now he was hurting us in the way only someone you love and who has loved you can hurt you.

I called the police.

"My stepdad is drunk and upset, and he just threw my brother out, and I'm stuck in my room with him smashing around outside my door."

"Can you get out of the house and go to a neighbour's house?"

"He's in the way between me and the front door."

"Can you go out a window?"

"I'm in a wheelchair. I wouldn't get very far without it."

Sirens blared.

The cops pounded on the front door. Tony's rage exploded at me. How the fuck could I have called the pigs on him. I was worthless. I was the lowest of low.

The cops shouted back. "Unlock the door or we'll break it down!"

I sat behind the door of my bedroom, staring at the yellow and orange floral 1960s wallpaper that I had hated every day we lived in this stupid house, with its stairs up to the front door and the nonexistent ramp that had been promised but was never actually built for me. I sat, waiting for things to escalate, waiting for this disaster to shape me, waiting to have survived this.

Tony shouted at me, "Come and open the door for your *friends.*"

He was conceding. I hadn't expected that.

He contained himself in the living room. I opened my bedroom door, crossed the dining room to the entryway, past where he paced, and unlocked the front door. I don't remember how Tony got outside. I don't remember the confrontation between him and the cops.

I have this one searing image.

Tony is kneeling on the sidewalk outside the house in full view of the neighbourhood. He has his hands cuffed behind his back. His head is bowed. Humiliated.

The adrenaline gave me clarity – I knew I was doing the right thing, and I retained the ability to act. It got me through the heat of the moment.

But it wouldn't last.

I have two very clear memories of my stepfather. The first is him waving me off on my first big adventure. The stretch of his body from his foot on the ground to his fingers spread out above him to make sure I could see him, to assure me that he loved me and would miss me everyday.

And the second is this: him on his knees, folded in on himself, crumpled. Betrayed – by me.

I never think of one moment without thinking of the other.

They charged him with unlawful confinement. Resisting arrest. They kept him in jail for long enough that my mom could sell the house. The house that was her dream come true, now derelict. She had to start over but not from scratch. My cautious, rule-abiding, fiscally anal mother was starting from a deficit of massive debt Tony had amassed.

She didn't waste a second. She rented a house, she paid off the debt, she set firm boundaries. Tony could not live with her while he was still drinking. They had date nights instead. His affection and tenderness resurfaced. But not his sobriety. He brought us gifts. Whatever he could scrounge and collect. And he respected the new conditions. He knew he'd hurt us and that he couldn't promise he wouldn't again.

In his gifts to me, I even imagined a kind of forgiveness. The you-did-what-you-had-to-do kind. He knew I'd done it for my mom. My mom made a point of saying so while he was still incarcerated. I didn't press charges. I just needed to buy my mom time, not punish Tony. All his jail time came from the charges the cops themselves laid against him.

I wanted to believe that he understood I had protected her when he couldn't. He could see she was doing better because of it. But I couldn't let myself acknowledge what I had given up to do it. A father's love and respect.

Tony died of an unintentional overdose on July 1, 2005. I walked to the church where the funeral was happening, but I couldn't take myself inside. My grief was so deep and complicated that I opted to feel nothing. I didn't want to be anywhere that could make me grieve. So I sat at the bottom of the staircase and closed myself off instead.

❦

I met Elliott at a meeting for writers. It was the first day of November in 2008, a very cold, dark, and wet month in Ontario. It was night, and the bus I had intended to take to get to the meeting refused to transport me. It was one with a few stairs into it, which is not an issue for me. I pull my chair up the stairs, sit in a seat, and tuck my chair against me. I take up no more room than a person with a stroller, and I'm safer than babies strapped into a wheeled devices and unable to remove themselves. But the driver refused, citing insurance policy restrictions. He threatened to call the police if I got on anyway. In the end, I relented. I called my mom to drive me out to the meeting instead.

When I told the story to some people I met that night, including my future ex-husband, Elliott, he advocated for the driver. "I'm sure he's telling the truth about their insurance not allowing you on the bus. What was he supposed to do?" he said, as though he was being reasonable and my hurt and my frustration was misplaced.

I held my ground, the unsettling feeling of being denied a bus ride carrying over to having to stand up for myself. "He could get into more legal trouble leaving me behind in the dark and the cold as much as he could for letting me on the bus. It also doesn't matter. Even if he's telling the truth, how can an insurance company say that a baby in a stroller is okay, but not someone like me? The risk factor is the same and the baby can't speak for itself. That driver said no, others say it's okay – how can I predict when I'll be allowed and when I won't? What does that tell you about the world I have to navigate? The effect on me is the same whether it's the driver's fault or not."

Elliott shrugged and then drove himself home.

A girl I had also just met accompanied me to the bus stop, understanding in an embodied and intuitive way that I needed someone with me to make going home normal and not a situation to cause anxiety.

Once a week, all through November, the little writing group met and talked about characters and plot development. I stopped trying to write fiction after six days of describing beautiful scenes and the appearance of a dryad and her not sexually intimate bond with a stag; there wasn't a shred of plot. I wasn't writing anything at all, but I continued to go to the meetings for the company. I started to spend time with Elliott outside of meetings.

The first meeting with him had been abrasive and unpleasant, and I had no physical attraction to him. Though it was confusing, I liked not being attracted. It made me feel safe. I could still have sex, the mechanics worked, and I didn't feel the terror or shame sexual attraction made me feel. I hadn't made the connections to my childhood medical procedures or the desexualizing with which I had been bombarded my whole life with. I could have sex so casually, it took me a long time to understand that I was deeply afraid of genuine intimacy.

CHAPTER FIVE

A godsend

El Camino de Santiago, Spain, April 2008

The Camino is a 750-kilometre pilgrimage through the northern countryside of Spain. Elliott and I started near the French border, at the edge of the Pyrenees, and walked six to twenty kilometres a day up and down mountainous, unpaved pathways not at all designed for wheelchairs. It was arduous, muddy – a lot like my childhood in the bush of Northern Ontario, except instead of the damp smell of black spruce, the air had the drier scent of eucalyptus.

Every town we passed through or stopped in had a Catholic church. Frequently they existed because of the Camino, for the benefit of (or to capitalize on) the countless pilgrims that had walked the same path through these towns since the 800s. No matter how small or rural the town, the church altar and the statues were usually gilded. It was beautiful if you didn't think about the conquests that led to the Spanish amassing so much gold they could afford to paint rural church altars in it. We stopped in every one. The churches often had spectacular lore of Camino miracles that proved the power of Santiago, the

Apostle James, whose remains were believed to be found in the early 800s somewhere in Galicia. When King Alfonso II heard about it, he had a large temple built at the site. Church building was the political currency at the time, and the Camino proved strategic as Christian pilgrims from all over Europe followed and settled along the route, building strong cultural ties across Europe that deterred the Moors from invasion. I was not impressed by Santiago's ability to help the Spanish win the war against the Moors, or to bring roasted chicken back to life, or to erase my debt of sin and reduce the amount of time I would have to spend in purgatory.

But there is a whisper of a story that before Alfonso and Santiago, well before the 8th century, the Camino actually marked a path that followed the Milky Way. Visible at night, directly overhead, pilgrims walked from the east to the west, all the way to what they called "Finistere," the end of the earth. Beyond: unknown, the land of the dead, unexplored open sea. The city that built up near Finistere as the Camino swelled the area's population is called Santiago de Compostela – *Compostela* meaning land of stars.

I liked the idea of walking for hours through forested trails between outposts of civilization. I wanted to know if my body could do it and what it would be like if it could. The churches were decadent, opulent, juxtaposed in the midst of farming communities. In Navarrete, the altar piece is renowned for its massive size, indulgent embellishment, and for being painted entirely in gold. We entered while a service was happening and joined in the reverence for a bit. Sitting outside after, Elliott – who I was dating – told me "God" had given him a message that he was the reason I was there. That it was his *purpose* to make it possible for me to be there. He was not even slightly religious. I guess he was trying to give his own thought a mystical weight he thought I might appreciate. But I felt more mocked than supported. Both for being disabled and for having an affinity for mysticism.

I had never seen examples of people who looked like me succeeding in any way as I grew up. All I saw were examples of people who looked like me being the trophies for the moral successes of able-bodied people. No successes and experiences that were owned by the disabled person. I had a strong and defensive desire to own my own experiences. I started to give him an undignified cold shoulder. I was testy in every conversation. I would have found a way to go without him. And I was sure I would have enjoyed it more if I had.

The trip had been my idea, my vision, my planning, and I was pushing myself up mountains and through forests. It's true that he had paid for the bulk of it; when the strap on my backpack broke, he carried it on his chest; and he never complained about the number of times I stopped to rest. He did complain about the time I let myself race down the first downhill we'd come across in a week. His argument was that he had walked *up* the mountains slowly to keep pace with me, I should have gone *down* slowly, to keep pace with him. I disagreed. Controlling a descent in a wheelchair is as physically strenuous as pushing uphill, because the tiny wrist muscles have to do all the work instead of powerful core and bicep muscles. Who stands with another person on wheels, poised at the top of a smooth hill, after *days* of uphill strain, and wants *more* strain as an expression of solidarity?

While none of his contributions seemed like enough to credit him with being the *reason* for the entire experience, the real problem was the fact that he even *wanted* credit – that credit was the measure of the experience for him.

The experience, for me, was the ghost of sun through mist in the mornings on our way through Rioja. Vineyard-scattered landscapes and manicured pathways for several kilometres outside of urban borders. The kink of anxiety as you leave a city boundary by foot or arm-powered wheel that unravels as you walk through wilderness and becomes an addictive elation at the sight of each encouraging sign that you are heading in the right direction, making progress toward the next town. He did not muse on these things.

Just outside Burgos, on April 13th – my birthday – we stopped at a rugged, though magical, albergue (the Spanish word for hostel). It was nestled into an endless undulation of green hills, invisible until you were at its door. It lacked electricity and running water, but possessed a ring of fairy stones in a nearby clearing of trees and a domed ceiling full of pagan symbolism, and goddesses painted all over the exterior. The lack of electricity meant, at night, the sky was lit up with stars. The lack of electricity also meant we were the only pilgrims there.

It had my name written all over it. A little bit fairy tale, a little forested, a lot in the middle of nowhere, and I had walked there on my own strength, which is exactly how you earn fairy tale blessings. Under the dome, the surfaces were littered with musical instruments, so I played a guitar, and the German and two Italians who ran the albergue made me a decadent birthday feast by candlelight. Risotto, roasted vegetables, tiramisu, and red wine. They sang happy birthday to me in several languages and three-part harmony. Meanwhile my godsent co-pilgrim entertained himself by doing the math on using a nearby mountain stream to generate a small amount of electricity.

The next day, I quit the Camino. Half-way to Finistere and Santiago de Compostela, in my own "land of stars." One of the Italian pilgrims drove us down the dirt roads we had only just walked, back to the bus station in Burgos. It was a lost cause. The easy explanation was my body quitting, but I knew it was my heart that was over it. I couldn't keep going with someone who saw himself as the defining principal in the whole quest and to whom I had absolutely no sensory connection, even as we were walking it together.

I let Elliott think I was giving up. He acted like he had won a competition I hadn't intended to enter.

"Just get me out of here," I said. "I want to wear a dress, get a stylish haircut." I wanted to pilgrimage myself into glamour. Eat a form of cheese not called Manchego. So we headed – for my first time – to Paris.

That April of 2007, several days after my twenty-seventh birthday, is maybe the first time I ever felt like a woman. Like the woman I had dreamed of becoming when I was a kid. We were in Paris, Elliott and I, for two days before we flew back to Canada. I posed in front of the Eiffel tower as Elliott took pictures. I felt beautiful and luminous, like the city itself made me glow from within. The first blush of feeling sexy. It was strange that Elliott would be the first to take a photo like that – I didn't connect the feeling with him. I think he understood it better than I would give him credit for, I was glad he had captured it, but I didn't share it with him.

CHAPTER SIX

When You Get What You Want
London, Ontario, Canada, November 2008

The first time Elliott told me he loved me, he told the back of my head. A month into hanging out, Elliott invited me to his penthouse apartment in Montreal for a weekend visit. Nothing physical had happened between us yet. I could feel the moment was coming when I would have to decide one way or the other if I was going to have sex with him. I knew he wanted to. I figured I'd decide in Montreal.

"So... do you want to sleep on the couch... or...?" he trailed off nervously that first night I arrived.

I can picture sitting on the IKEA futon with the faux leather covering under the windows looking out over Montreal from the peak of Vieux Port. The kitchen pot lights were dimmed. The walls were bare. He was proud of the decorative additions his sister and mother had made to make the apartment feel homier, but I thought it felt uninhabited – without even that impersonal yet luxurious and welcoming feel that a well-decorated hotel room can achieve.

When my genitals soaked in arousal during fairly routine medical procedures, no one had explained that it was normal for your body to respond to stimulation, regardless of your brain or your heart's opinion on the matter. No one had explained *stimulation* to me at all. My earliest memories of this weird arousal started when I was eight. I remember the dreams. Sexual dreams that would shake me awake with shame and bladder spasms. I don't know where I got the explicit images from; I don't know if sex had been mentioned at all. I knew enough to feel there was something wrong with me.

Frequently, gloved hands spread my labia, brushing and pressing against me firmly and softly. They would lubricate a thin plastic catheter, sometimes they would get close enough in order to see my urethra that I could feel warm breath on my exposed and now moist flesh. I knew it was wrong to feel all this tingling and urge to squirm. It felt meaningless before puberty, it was a painless procedure. But when I got older, some part of me, it seemed... liked it? No, I couldn't allow that. But I couldn't hate it either – that would mean admitting it felt good. I wanted to go back to meaningless. I couldn't stop my body from glistening, so I learned to disconnect from it. I put my heart away. No feelings, just body. Just a surge of meaningless heat from my genitals to the pulse in my neck. And then I forgot how to make heart and brain and arousal mesh again.

I agreed to join Elliott in his bed. He was shy, physically awkward mixed with respect, so I initiated and directed the sex we had that night. He had stamina and I had no inhibitions. I didn't have to feel attraction for my body to respond with arousal, I'd had enough confusing medical exams to know that. We fucked in every position I could physically get into while in bed, and then we tried several more in the bathtub.

"I want to quit my job and just have sex with you every day," he said to me, his face sopping and resting momentarily on the inside of my thigh. I loved that. I had sexually satisfied and exhausted a man.

The next morning, Elliott rolled over to spoon me and said, "I have to tell you something." I froze, expecting the worst. He prepared himself and, in a voice muted with thick saliva, he said, "I'm completely in love with you." I stayed stiff. I had just been thinking I didn't like the way the sheets smelled sour, I didn't like the way our body odours mixed. I wanted out of the closeness of our bodies. Also, I was supposed to be unlovable. This was... new territory.

"I suspected it before, but I wanted to wait until we had sex to be sure, sometimes it can just wear off after you... get what you want," he explained.

I didn't say it back. I wasn't in love with him. But I was going to have my first real, in-love-with-me boyfriend at age twenty-six, and I was very excited about that.

I told myself that the lack of sexual attraction I felt for him actually elevated our relationship. We connected in other, more sustainable ways. We could talk to each other about anything, including money and power. He never once bristled or winced or attempted to shame me for my intelligence. He liked that he could tell me anything without having to edit his thoughts or slow down. He liked that I was an artist, was frustrated when he felt I wasn't pursuing my music, or any of my skills and passions. He was eager to invest the money I needed to develop my craft and realize my visions.

It was clear from our first interaction that my experience, my disability, was irrelevant to him. On the one hand, he treated me like a person. On the other hand, he did not take the effect my disability had on me into consideration. Even when it was his attitude about disability affecting me. With him I had unprecedented levels of financial security, which allowed me to explore my art and go on wild adventures. It also allowed me to picture a future I could reasonably count on. I could spread out across time. If you are fixed in the present by some kind of pain and if it lasts long enough, the future becomes uncertain and you contract around what you know, what is immediate. For a while, the future felt like it could be as secure as the present. It felt spacious.

During our relationship, Elliott paid to upgrade the metal of my new wheelchair to lighter, state-of-the-art titanium alloy but then refused to have hand controls installed in his car so I could learn to drive. In the end, it was much like the arbitrary-seeming decision-making process the government used to decide what it would fund and not fund, or being at the mercy of which bus driver would let me on the bus and which would not. There were so many things I could not know before I tried to go where I wanted to go. I was used to handling that kind of uncertainty. What the government considered necessities of daily living and what it considered lifestyle preferences made you aware that the only lifestyle a disabled person was allowed to prefer was one of extreme dependence. At least, under my ex's purview, I could *prefer* to travel and create. He valued, in a way society did not, me as an artist, me as an independent woman.

Once, as we were thinking of moving in together, I had an appointment with my case worker. I was on a disability pension that covered my rent and medical expenses. She told me that if Elliott made more than a certain amount of money, it would affect my benefits.

"But what does his income have to do with my medical expenses?" I asked.

"If he makes a certain amount of money, you don't qualify for our insurance," the case worker responded mechanically.

"But we would just be living together. Our expenses would be still separate. Cutting off my benefits because he's around implies that he would have to be responsible for my expenses."

"Well, yes. If he doesn't want to support you, he shouldn't be with you," she said, tired of the conversation, the philosophical question of my worth as an individual settled by the policies she enforced without questioning.

That's what being disabled in a relationship meant. On a practical level, dating a girl in a wheelchair meant you had to agree to shoulder the expense of her. You had to understand that the reason she was expensive was because she was not supporting herself, not contributing, not valuable, a burden. Who would still choose to be with her?

I was furious at the situation. I was devastated by it. If our relationship progressed, I would not be his equal partner but his literal dependent. If I insisted on my government-assisted independence, our relationship couldn't progress. It became representational of all possible relationships. I could be independent, or I could rely on a single person to handle all my needs. They would get to decide what my needs were, how to meet them, and what I should do with myself once they were met. Were these reasonable things to trust your romantic partner with? How could you determine whether or not someone was worthy of a trust like that?

In the end, we compromised: we rented an apartment for him that was closer to mine. I was relaxed when I was with him. There was no attraction to intimidate me, there was a distance between us that soothed me. The security I felt in our relationship was its own kind of intimacy, equal to an emotional intimacy, I thought. I relied on him, and he enabled me. What more could I want from a husband? I respected him for his skills, for his intelligence, for his logical generosity. Attraction was fickle, yes. But it was rare for me in general, and, anyway, didn't everyone say that you should marry someone you never got tired of talking to because sexual lust would inevitably wear off? I felt wise and self-possessed in my relationship. I didn't feel connected, but we understood each other and accepted each other in a meaningful way. I told myself that was a kind of falling in love – or at least, a way of falling in love for someone like me. When he asked, I said yes, I would marry him.

We were engaged for weeks, maybe longer, before I managed to convince him he needed to tell his parents – who still didn't even know I existed.

I had nudged him many times to tell them. He would shrug me off, saying his family just didn't talk about this kind of thing. But they talked often enough, it seemed to me, and anyway an engagement is exactly the "kind of thing" all families talk about. So I kept nudging. Looking back, I'm astounded at my gentleness. Not as a point of pride. But as an example of how no amount of intellectual capacity can stand in for personal experience when it comes to some parts of life. I knew that when you were engaged, you told your family. But I had no other experience with romantic relationships, so my re-creation of it was cold and practical: Immediate family should know. I expected him to tell his family out of respect and to avoid conflict if they found out too late. I might have asked him if he was happy to be marrying me, but maybe I didn't. It wasn't a key issue to me. I didn't expect him to be thrilled to be engaged to me.

I was sitting on the carpet of his unfurnished living room while he made the call.

"Mom, I'm engaged," Elliott blurted out.

I could hear her surprised shriek through the phone.

"She's in a wheelchair, she doesn't work. We met at a writing club," he said all in the same, rushed breath.

Later I asked him why his sole description of me was my wheelchair and my employment status.

"I just want to get it out of the way in case someone has a problem with it. They can't use it against me if I've already brought it up."

It seemed fair. He had already asked me to marry him, was already financially supporting me, did he also have to be bouncing down the halls with uncontainable excitement too? I chalked it up to his natural reserve and unemotional affect and moved on, pleased that he had completed the appropriate gesture.

Years later I learned the word "ableism." I learned it from other disabled people on social media. I reviewed the early parts of my marriage with the new lens and considered that, along with the stability he brought to my life, he was a reflection of the ableism I had internalized. In almost any other area of my life, I assumed I had every right to participate, even when I was told I didn't. I fought for my place. But when it came to romantic relationships, I had, without even knowing it, assumed he was making an exception for me. Taking a specific risk that other people in relationships don't have to take. And he agreed with my assessment. Agreeing on that made it feel like we were on the same page. Like we were making good and smart and reasoned choices.

We were engaged to be married and ostensibly in love. He happened to have a twelve-hour-a-day kind of job, to which he was devoted. Meanwhile, I travelled on my own and kept my own apartment. We had compatible lifestyles. I repeatedly wondered why, then, I was so emotionally unsatisfied. It's bewildering to me now, but at the time, I genuinely had no idea.

I put myself under immense pressure to be *worth* the risk. I focused on that and never considered whether or not it was true that I was a romantic burden – that no matter how cool or sexy or fun or intelligent I was, no one would want me. I put myself in the position of having to talk someone into letting me be with them. It felt weird, of course, but it felt weird to talk people into letting me do anything – the more regular the thing I wanted to do, the weirder it was. Weird didn't mean wrong. And I was determined. I could do this. My mindset around romance by the time I met Elliott was: Let me do this! It distorted everything and was exhausting and accompanied by an outsized sense of foreboding responsibility. If I was talking him into it, I'd better be right about it being a good idea. That made me so uncomfortable, anxious, and self-conscious as it always did, whenever I had to talk my way into a situation everyone was sure I shouldn't be in – I thought it was responsible for all the other feelings of discomfort marrying him brought me. I expected it to pass as things worked out. Instead, my supply of self-esteem ran bone dry for years at a time from the effort of trying to make myself "worth it." The unresolvable conundrum was that even if I could achieve "it," I could never know what being worth it even looked like. It changed with every person.

Every relationship had a different risk assessment. Within a single relationship, criteria shifted like seasons.

It didn't occur to me as a young girl to question the assertion that I was unlovable. I had too many reasons to accept it. The question I *was* asking was: How do I live in a world where this is true and still enjoy it? What do I do with all this passion and sexuality and love burgeoning in me? Watch porn and read romance novels? Forever? Big questions for a young girl who hadn't even had a first date yet. I didn't have any sex at all until my late twenties, after which I was immediately torn between how much I liked it and how confusing and lonely it felt. And then I married the man who liked it when people congratulated him on how generous, nice, and brave he was to be with me. The man who told me he didn't see my disability; it was like I wasn't disabled at all. I agreed with him. I believed that I couldn't have needs if I wanted to be loved, and what was a disability but an unrelenting neediness. So I couldn't be disabled. That was what it would take to be loved.

All love was a risk, I could see that was true for everyone. But was it true, that loving me required a *heroic* degree of risk? Was it true that love was too much for me to really handle?

CHAPTER SEVEN

To Marry a Forest
Middlesex County, Ontario, Canada, May 2009

It was my idea to plant trees at our wedding. Elliott found us a plot of land owned by a woman passionate about historical preservation and indigenous reforestation. She found us grants for supplies, and I connected with a childhood friend of mine who was then the head of ReForest London. We bussed our sixty or so wedding guests, dressed in galoshes and jeans, to the site and gave them wheelbarrows and saplings. We then dug in the earth until we had planted more than eighty Ontario-native trees and shrubs.

I spent my wedding morning on my knees, drenched in earth, mud caked into my wheels, using my wheelchair as a wheelbarrow for saplings. At the time, I turned my nose up at the poufy wedding dresses and the long stroll down an aisle drenched in flower petals. I felt indifferent to the pageantry, to the general idea of a wedding day at all. I thought it was because I was "too cool." I thought it was because I was focusing on what really mattered. I still believe that my tree-planting wedding was a special day of community and sincerity. But it wasn't true that I hated wedding pageantry and glamour. I just didn't believe it could be for me. I felt self-conscious when I imagined myself in a cascading dress. The tearful eyes of wedding guests as I rolled down the aisle. The sentiments felt out of control and disproportionate to how I felt about getting married, which was more of a pragmatic decision for me. It strikes me now, especially knowing how exhilarated I am by fashion and drama, that when I pictured the dresses and dances and poses for photos, it wasn't really myself I couldn't imagine, it was Elliott. I couldn't see how he would hold me or be with me in those moments. I could wear a massive tulle sculpture and place myself on an altar next to him if I wished, but he would be standing awkward and self-conscious next to me, not proudly and glamorously being with me. Thoughts of what life and love and family meant to me swirled unresolved. I wanted him to be comfortable that day. I wanted to be comfortable with him that day. I did not love him glamorously, so I asked for trees.

Barbara, who owned the land we planted on, named the reforested plot of land Erin's Dell. Not the Wedding Dell or Elliott and Erin's Dell. A delicate omen that the marriage would not last, but something beautiful and sustainable would.

Three years into our marriage, my husband moved to New York to take a job he told me he would never take. At the time, we were living on Salt Spring Island in British Columbia. When he left, I stayed. Every other weekend, I travelled from one coast to the other, from island to island, so I could spend four days in NYC. I hired a woman to help me run errands and to walk my dog Foxy, now that my husband was not there. She brought fancy hats for us to wear to the grocery store. My very first Instagram photos were of moments with her. Bowls of berries she picked for me from her garden, rose petals on the threshold of my home to roll over when I returned home from New York.

I had a dream to marry a forest. I wanted to be a hub, a creative whirlpool, where all my friends and their friends could come and find respite and inspiration. Trees made me feel safe, they ignited my senses with their seasons, their sway in the wind, their fragrances. And I wanted to share that magic with others. When we agreed to move to the island, Elliott shared the dream. We called it our "summer camp." The feeling I wanted to recreate was the outdoorsy friendship-filled experience summer camp was for so many kids, but without mandatory activities. Elliott could run the tech start-up he had always dreamed of, and I could host an impromptu and ongoing salon. But after the initial excitement wore off, Elliott fretted over the remoteness of the island, which was only accessible by ferry. How would he attract programmers? Could he get funding? His worries were what led him to take the job in New York. Once he did, I realized that the impulse to take a secure placement with solid pay and prestige had always been there. Maybe he wanted to be the kind of person who could follow a dream, find solutions to problems on the fly, persist through uncertain periods and have fun all the way through. But in reality, the closer to that we got, the more anxiety he expressed.

It was after he left, a short time after we settled into our house, that friends started arriving and bringing their friends. I'd have long conversations with people I had never met before, hosting them in my home. I would hear them sigh, take in lungfuls of pine-scented air, and relax a little deeper into themselves. Local friends filled my house with their live music, their fresh produce from island farms, bouquets of wildflowers from their walks in the woods. The island had several professional theatres, hundreds of artists' studios. My friends and I would go to the docks on the nude lake and sunbathe, drive in the dark with our eyes out for the ubiquitous and adorably treacherous wild deer, and, in every season, the most handsome trees I had ever met.

It was my favourite year of being married.

I arrived in British Columbia with a passion for being an aerialist that I'd caught during a weekend workshop just before moving with Elliott. I found it particularly magical that the small island I had chosen as my home also happened to have an aerial studio where I could continue to learn aerial arts. The instructors who taught me my first weekend workshop in London had all the fun, playing with the massive upper body strength I had. Victoria, who owned the aerial studio, and I had all the challenges of making progress by facing my weaknesses.

When I wasn't training on aerial silks, I was taking acting workshops with Act III Studios. We did intense scene studies. We did practices to get into our bodies. To let our emotions move freely through us, out of the dialogue and into the interaction with our partner.

During one of these workshops, my partner and I had a scene in which I played a social worker and she was the mother of a child I had placed out of her care. My scene partner was a tall and gorgeous woman, but I was the character with power in the scene. At one tense moment, after she had been towering over me, shouting down into my face, I learned toward her instead of away and she relented, moved away from me. I hopped up on the desk to deliver my line, and she slumped in the seat. I was towering over her. None of it had been planned. Through the exercises, the breathing, the focus, and the connection between us, it was just how we managed to move the energy around the stage. I had negotiated, in character, an exchange of power, using body language and timing, between me and an able-bodied scene partner. I was so used to the alienation and disempowerment that came from my body speaking a foreign and unknown language to the people around me. As an actor, as a performer, I became intimately close with people who spoke a version of my body language close enough to understand each other without interpretation.

And then Elliott cheated.

About a year into our bi-coastal living, he had an affair.

He had met the other woman at work. He emailed me from New York to ask me if I was comfortable with them going on a personal trip to Quebec City together. I wasn't. But I said I was.

As their relationship developed, Elliott shared the details of their conversations, an instinct that something was up nagged at me. The frustrating part of intuition is how it doesn't allow you to show your work. You know the answer, but you can't prove how you got to it. When it comes to the things people think or feel or do when you're not around, you can't prove it. So, who do you trust? What your gut tells you, or what your husband does?

I was sure she was trying to have an affair with him. She once asked him if she could tell him something that he wouldn't share with me. He told me that he'd told her that it was okay, she was allowed privacy. I told him that I didn't think she had a secret. It felt like a test – to whom would he be loyal? – and he had given her the answer she wanted. We fought about that. He felt that I was being jealous and suspicious and competitive. That it didn't matter if she wanted to have an affair or not if I trusted him. He was just being a good friend and she had no one else she could talk to.

I countered that it did matter whether or not she was trying to have an affair with him, because what kind of husband wanted to be good friends with someone who was trying to do something to hurt his wife? It hurt that her feelings were more important to him than mine. Maybe I was jealous, suspicious, competitive, but wasn't I allowed to be?

"Your feelings don't hurt you the way other people's do, you're stronger than us," I remember him saying to me. He was saying things I had said to myself in my own mind. I had approached the entire marriage with the objective of having no needs, but hearing it out loud, now that I was hurt? Elliott, and therefore I, sounded ridiculous.

I also suspected that he knew what she wanted, and that he wanted it too, without having to admit that he did. Elliott and I were not sexually compatible. We never had been. I had encouraged him in the past to find outlets for his sexual needs. I wanted him to be satisfied. I encouraged him again.

If you want to, have sex with her. I meant it as an expression of support, a way of relieving the pressure and tension building between us. I didn't think of how it could be felt as a rejection: *I don't want to fuck you, if she does, go for it!*

He didn't want to have sex with her, it wasn't even about that, he claimed. It was about me trusting him. He wanted me to listen to the ins and outs of their power dynamic and psychological intimacy to prove something to himself about his integrity. Maybe he just wanted me to be jealous. But I felt too guilty about not being attracted to him to worry about jealousy. I also had no interest in her – if she had gained my admiration in some way, maybe I would feel jealous. But she was predictable and plain and I was being manipulated from both sides. My deeply ingrained default when I feel manipulated is to concede, withdraw, goodbye. I wanted my marriage to be an emotionally safe and reliable environment, and I knew communication was an important part of that, so I kept overriding my urge to shut down. But we were never communicating. Competing versions of reality, an ever-changing objective, arguments like labyrinths, like halls of mirrors. Exhausted from fighting about it but not ready to give up the marriage, I faked trusting him.

He was not the kind of guy who accidentally had sex with someone, he asserted.

"It just... happened. By accident," he said.

He never *actually* confessed to the affair. He didn't have to. He'd arranged to visit me on the island instead of my usual bi-weekly visit to him in NYC. I knew before he arrived and I brought it up. He blamed it on the stress of the extra money it was costing to live on opposite coasts. He blamed me.

"Please be angry with me," he pleaded. "If you're not angry, then there's nothing left." I think he wanted me to shout about how hurt I was, to put him in the position of getting to reassure me that he still loved me and wanted me, or the position of labelling me as crazy. Maybe he wanted to provoke a strong reaction to know that he could, or to feel like I cared. But angry gave them power over you, angry confessed that they'd hurt you. I didn't trust him with that now. I was angry with myself instead. I had been so right about her motivations, and even his likely responses, yet repeatedly set my own perception aside to try to see it his way. I had forced myself to trust him with the integrity of our relationship, ruining my peace of mind by trying to find a balance between his version of events and mine. But what could I have done differently? If I had said I wasn't comfortable with them going to Quebec at the beginning, he just would have called me jealous sooner. When I tried to tell him to stop giving me updates of their relationship, he accused me of abandoning him. There was no victory in being right, no point in arguing about it anymore, there was just a sinking feeling of my respect for him draining out of me. I did not want to know him better than he knew himself if all that meant was I could predict how he would hurt me. I told him that I couldn't see a way forward that didn't involve him getting some kind of therapy. He needed to take responsibility for his desires and his actions. After a few days of hearing me repeat that, he told me I had punished him enough and it was time to move on. The contradiction that he wanted me to show him my anger but didn't want to address my emotional needs made me wonder, could all this be intentional?

"Do you know how this feels to me?" I asked him plaintively when he refused couple's counselling, solo counselling, to stop working with his mistress, or any of the things I had asked him for in the name of reconciliation.

"Yes. I can imagine it would hurt," he said, releasing me from the responsibility of single-handedly reconciling anything between us. He didn't care enough to do anything differently. A strange simplicity broke through. He was right, it was time to move on, but not as a couple the way Elliott meant it. It was time to reconcile with myself.

Instead of getting a divorce, Foxy and I moved to New York full time to alleviate the financial stress of living in two separate places. I knew my relationship with Elliott was over, but I was still in love with my life. People lived inside dead marriages all the time. And he was right, I was stronger than him. I could hold off on my forest dream, I could live with trees in the future, once he had exhausted himself in the corporate world. At least in New York I could continue with acting, performing, and aerial training. There was a class about ten blocks from my apartment that I began attending twice a week. That's where I met Laura von Holt.

Laura is a cheerful blonde actress, writer, and businesswoman with an independent and tenacious streak as intense as my own. We clicked instantly.

During class, Laura and I fell into an ongoing banter, parrying little jokes we'd stretch out into mini scenes. We were entertaining ourselves, and then it was entertaining to others. Organically, our banter turned us into character versions of ourselves. Her character was sweet, bubbly, and affable. Mine was severe and sexy. Our friendship was its own character in our bits. Early on, we were asked to host one of the monthly circus cabaret shows in the city. The circus schools offered opportunities for the local talent and its students to perform as part of a variety and talent show once a month. Generally, hosts took a couple notes of the acts they were introducing, told some jokes, and got on with it. The first time Laura and I hosted, we wrote whole skits and wove them into our introductions of each act. One month, we commandeered the entire thing, recruited a couple circus performers from our community and staged a competition to find our number-one fan.

After that show, it occurred to Laura and me that we could do circus acts and write skits. We should just introduce ourselves and star in the whole show. Most professional aerialists support themselves by working corporate gigs and galas. However, in my experience, companies would not hire a disabled performer unless they were hiring her to specifically give an inspirational performance. I couldn't just be talented, I had to account for my wheelchair and how that would make people in the audience feel. This was true for a lot of my career options which either were inaccessible or the hiring process was impeded by outright discrimination. The artists I knew supported themselves as waitresses, working at Starbucks, in retail. Jobs I could not do. I could see myself on stage, but I couldn't see the practical steps toward supporting myself as an artist. My strategy was to find ways to put myself in the oncoming traffic of art and hope something struck. My skill became creating opportunities out of what looked like just having fun. It also turned out to be Laura's skill. We became an aerial comedy duo.

CHAPTER EIGHT

An Inspiration
New York, New York, U.S., 2014-2015

Laura and I called ourselves Flaming Mermaid Broken Star. We performed our first show at Dixon Place, a theatre space in New York whose stage is wheelchair accessible. We rigged two aerial silks from the lighting grid, and we wrote, choreographed, and performed our sold-out debut: "Flaming Mermaid Broken Star's Famous World of Wonders." We invented the concept of "aerial feminism" – centring in our act talk about princesses and power and sex appeal and friendship. She was affable and sweet and bubbly. I was severe. And sexy.

During our introduction, Laura would be talking and all of a sudden I would interrupt her, saying I felt like people had noticed there was something different about me. And I wasn't comfortable proceeding without acknowledging it. I didn't want there to be anything uncomfortable between me and the audience.

And Laura would encourage me to go on.

"As you can see, I am using... a microphone," I would say, pinching the strap of my top and exaggerating my voice into the lav mic pinned there. Everyone could see my wheelchair, no one could see the lav mic.

Everyone would laugh. And Laura would nod seriously. "It's because I'm a sex icon," I'd say.

I would explain that to be a sex icon you have to do a lot of smouldering and kegel exercises, so my core was constantly engaged with these activities, and that made it hard to project my voice. Therefore, I needed audio augmentation.

"Thank you for explaining that to us," Laura would say in a dreamy, sincere voice, projecting at a fine volume without using a microphone.

"Yes, I'm a sex icon because I care."

Later in the show, Laura would pull out one of those Barbie-brand microphones from the 1980s. It was a giant, ridiculous pink-and-blue beast that amplifies voices using reverberating metal coils.

"I want to be more like you," she would offer sweetly.

Despite our intellectually super smooth act, being a sex icon had started with an inside joke.

During our training, I frequently showed up in aerial class with another story of someone who was so proud of me for being outside, crossing the street on my own. One day, I remember a stranger on the street actually grabbing the frame of my chair and kneeling in front of me to have "a moment" over how much I inspired them. I remember recounting the story and someone responding, "But they're being nice. You *are* inspiring." And me replying, somewhat indignantly, "If someone you didn't know grabbed you and forced you to talk to them, would you care what they wanted to tell you?"

I was furious at how impossible it seemed to communicate how violating and assaulting it felt. Likewise I found it painful and alienating to realize that the people around me, people I thought of as peers and friends, didn't seem to think it mattered whether or not I was awarded the same basic level of respect and autonomy they expected for themselves.

One day, Laura and I were walking home from class when she said, "I have been thinking about it. And I've solved your life. The next time someone says, OH MY GOD! You are SO inspiring! Just look them dead in the eye and say, 'Yes, but do you think I'm sexy?'"

It was genius. And liberating. And so dark.

When people were interrupting me to tell me how inspiring I was, they were objectifying me. I was experiencing what other women experience when they get cat-called and then told they should be flattered instead of offended.

Instead of using the line in real life, Laura and I used the concept in our shows. In place of ever referencing my disability or wheelchair, I referred instead to my sex appeal. I was making the point, through the character of a Sex Icon, that my wheelchair is as superficial a defining quality of me as sex appeal is for any woman.

It was also powerful to superimpose a wheelchair and sex appeal. A wheelchair is considered the universal symbol of powerlessness and confinement. Sex appeal is considered a form of power and liberation. To make them interchangeable opened up the realm of narrative possibilities. You don't *overcome* sex appeal, you use it. I do the same with my wheelchair. I would do the same, as an artist, with my disability.

Over time, Sex Icon became more of a metaphor than a character, and the people reading along on instagram and coming on my adventures started to use it to refer to moments of pleasure, moments of confidence and well-being, moments of solitude and self-awareness. It morphed into something rich and complex through the relationship and intimacy with my audience. Being in control of my own narrative wasn't about a rigidity or resistance as much as it was about authenticity and relationship. To be changed and to influence change.

Sexuality is internal, but it is also interactive. If your wheelchair defines you to others, but not to yourself, how do you get to interact sexually and romantically to figure that part of it out without surrendering to the preferences of someone whose fetish is for a wheelchair? Being a Sex Icon gave me the chance to have those interactions on my own terms, facilitated by my skill as a performer, between me and an entire audience of people.

As a child, I was set up to defend a sexuality I didn't know existed. I wasn't just uncomfortable with being catheterized by others because I was independent, I was *sexually* uncomfortable. But I had no concept for that.

As a teenager I had not shaken the feeling that my arousal was a bad reaction to being touched, a reckless and uncontrolled force. And so, I was scared. What would happen to me if I let go? How badly could I be hurt? Would I come back together again? My fear of sex overrode my hormones.

And what to do with the hideous taboo of having sex with a disabled person? If anyone who wanted to have sex with me was a sick pervert, what did that make me for wanting to have sex with them? The most logical solution at the time was to not feel attracted to anyone. I had no answers for any of my questions about what I wanted and what I liked, and the process of discovering answers for myself would involve actually having sex and dating people I clearly couldn't trust.

But, as an adult in the structural safety of an open marriage, I was living in an era of sexual empowerment for women. And I was living in New York City. I could have the sex I wanted, as much as I wanted – the opportunity for every kind of sex was endless. Opportunities were themselves endless. I could have cheesecake and warm cookies delivered to my apartment at three in the morning. I could have Tinder deliver sex just as conveniently. This would be my liberation from my sex fears, I thought. I would take all this Sex Icon power and confidence and be promiscuous.

Yet, when one of my lovers called me a whore, I was jolted. I felt no shame over the sex. But it wasn't worth it. I was spending all this time with men doing this thing that still had a serious edge for me, and some of the men could turn out to be the kind who call women whores. I didn't know them, these men. I didn't really like them. My favourite moments were always on the sidewalk at dawn, freshly returned to myself. It was like after a doctor's appointment, that feeling of becoming myself again after being an object on an examining table. I didn't want to stay in these lovers' beds or see them again – the thrill of the flirting was potent, racing up to the edge of what I feared so indulgently, but the sex was just... sex. And I was still unsatisfied.

"What do I want?" I asked Laura as I shook in bewildered frustration and recounted the whore story. We were in a dark bar across 14th Street from Stuyvesant Town, where I was living. We were sipping drinks through straws with hula girls on them.

"I think you want feelings with your sex," Laura said with the kind of compassion that allows for something to be both completely obvious, even simple to one person, while remaining a total mystery to someone else.

I immediately recoiled. Sex without feelings was free, cool, more empowering. I wanted to want that. It came to me so easily. Why couldn't it be enough? She was right, but if I accepted that was what I wanted, then I'd be going all the way back, starting over from the beginning. Sex was serious. Intimacy scared me. Who could I trust with all that, and how would I know?

"I think you need some parenting," Laura said sympathetically. "This is the kind of thing you learn from a good dad."

Laura has a good dad. A quiet man who is a force of integrity and patience. A cowboy with a mustache and exciting gentleness. The kind of man who teaches you important things about men and women by his steady presence and how he treats your mother. Meanwhile, I had deadbeats as far as the eye could see.

"Can I have an imaginary dad?" I asked.

"Yeah!" Laura said, her eyes lighting up, feeling a fun imagination game coming on. We love to roleplay; it's the basis of our friendship.

"Okay... I think I'd like to be raised by a Viking sea god."

"Oh, that's good! You definitely have mythical parentage." Laura bounced in her seat and made fatherly pronouncements at me in a thunderous, god-like voice. "You want to fall in love, daughter," she boomed, her eyes bulging out with exaggerated seriousness.

My grandmother's parents were Norwegian farmers who immigrated to American farmland, where my grandmother was born. I had always wanted to go to Norway. Shortly after this conversation with Laura, I booked a trip and spent a continuous stretch of days on trains from Oslo to Bodø and back, communing with my imaginary daddy about the self-esteem I had seriously neglected and the new experience of romantic feelings I wanted to experience. For days, I watched streams of mountain run-off streak through tundra and lakes of a deep aqua colour. I breathed in forests and fjords. It was an immense landscape, majestic enough to contain my entire lifetime of longing and disappointment and not be bowed or depleted. In the end, I felt sturdy and well-fathered. I was ready for Paris – this time, alone.

CHAPTER NINE

The Lovers
Paris, France, July 2015

In Paris, I stayed in an Airbnb with a tiny, Parisian elevator I had to dismantle my wheelchair to fit into. The wheel shaft pressed into my thigh while I popped off the wheels and balanced myself around the separated parts for the ride. Tiny circular bruises dotted my leg from my knee to my hip by the time my visit was over.

One of my roommates told me that her favourite park in the city was the Palais-Royal. I was sitting there, eating sushi under a wall of pink roses, when the lovers joined me. They sat across from me and pulled plastic containers of food brought from home out of a canvas grocery bag. He had a long, dark beard and hair that you could tell was thick even though it was buzzed. He was broad in his white t-shirt and loose shorts and his forearms and calves were tattooed. Her light brown hair was pulled into a messy top knot, similar to the one I had pulled mine into when I chose the bench facing the sun.

She tucked her container back into their bag and put her head down in his lap as he finished his sandwich. It took some wiggling for them to get comfortable. She loosened the ties of her purple paisley halter top, and he slipped his hand under the light fabric and cupped her whole breast with his hand, resting his forearm across her torso and leaning sideways toward her.

She murmured up at him, and he cradled her head with his other hand, and she closed her eyes for a nap.

I lay back, propping my head up on the seat of my cushion. The sun prickled the skin on my shins, the folds of my bare stomach, along my cheekbones. The heat pulled my skin tight with a slight sting and made it slick with sweat. I undid the ties of my butterfly halter top and folded the top edge lower on my chest so the sun could slip his hand closer to my breast. My hidden skin flushed. I was doused with longing and the scent of rose petals in the humidity, a musky garden-and-lust smell. I closed my eyes for a nap.

The sun was coming from a tilt when I roused from my nap. It had been directly overhead when I first arrived, that's how long I had been there. Bright clouds passed across the sky, playing dimmer switches with the sun's intensity. One was especially perfect, outlined in blazing white with rays spilling out over the edges and reaching across a doubtless blue sky. My phone had died a while into my lounging so I couldn't take photos of it. Instead, I pulled out my journal to describe it.

The pages were damp and wrinkled from being pressed between the back of the bench and the side of my sweat-soaked body.

Across from me, the lovers were shifting. She rolled onto her side facing him, her face nestled against his stomach. They were making each other giggle. Pigeons cooed under my bench, which was very low to the ground and rounded instead of "L"

shaped. It was meant to cradle whoever sat in it. Meant to encourage one to take whatever time it took to truly relax.

I sat up to write and pressed my top to my chest by leaning
forward against my knee. One thin strap fell loose down my
back and the other trailed along my shoulder, slipping forward
and pooling at the crest of my breast against my thigh.

The clouds were still toying with the sun's mood. One moment it was pressing into me with urgent lust and then, just as
suddenly, falling back into a calmer affection.

The lovers broke apart. He lit a cigarette, and she ate from a
container of cut fruit.

I was thirsty and heat-tired, too, and there was only me to
get water, to smooth the stray hairs back from my cheeks and
forehead where they had stuck from sweat.

The lovers gazed at each other, eyes soft-focused and quiet.
She leaned forward. He puckered his lips and shot a stream of
water at her chest from between his teeth. She tilted away, startled and laughing. He smirked, took another sip, and sprayed
her again. This time, she welcomed it, lifting her chin to let the
water hit her chest and throat.

Then they left.

Paris is for lovers. But I didn't have a lover. My husband had
never been my lover. He'd been my sex partner. The men I was
sleeping with in NYC were sex partners. I had never had a lover.
Elliott told me once that it was unreasonable for me to want sex
to mean something, to be more than just a physical activity, to
achieve an emotional act of connection, and I believed him. I
was having orgasms, wasn't I? That was enough.

I was unsatisfied but resigned. Then, in a park in Paris, a
pair of lovers and their unselfconscious intimacy startled a moment of self-honesty: I was hungry to touch and be touched like

that, for an everyday passion with someone. Perhaps precisely because of the years of sex without connection, I understood something more subtle about the intimacy I was seeing. Like a symphony made powerful because of the silences between sound, my marriage was a silence and their affection was a warm sound that resonated through it, goosebumps on flesh, knowing without words. I could understand the language of their bodies. I irrevocably understood that I could not speak to Elliott that way, and he couldn't speak that way to me. Instead of painful envy, though, I had clarity.

It wasn't a hopeless fantasy. It wasn't at all unreasonable. Watching the lovers made me realize that while I had never let anyone tell me I couldn't play on monkey bars or travel the world or speak my mind, I had let anyone who ever had the slightest inclination tell me I could not love and be loved as fully and deeply as I desired. I was so scared of the pain love could cause that taking my unlovability as truth was a relief. I accepted a life without deep intimacy and made my choices accordingly. And I had made one very massive mistake as a result. I was hiding from myself in a marriage to a man I did not truly love. It wasn't Elliott that was hurting or disappointing me, it was being so disconnected from myself. If I wanted to fill the gnawing loneliness, if there was going to be any chance of true love, it wasn't a better love affair that I needed – it was a more truthful relationship with myself. I would have to risk everything, throw myself into total uncertainty, face the final fear. The scene of the lovers' affection was a touchstone, a hope, and a motivation. I kept it vivid in my mind.

I got back from Paris with a broken wheel. The bearing shattered, and the wheel tilted inside the fork. It was like pushing a grocery cart – if that grocery cart was also my body. I expected to be able to order new parts and fix it. But in the meantime, I was aware of the metaphor in my struggle to get anywhere. In the damage to my body. In Paris, I had flowed. And the flow made the idea of desire and a new beginning beautiful and empowering, and likewise it made the necessity of a divorce a straightforward next step. All these things had seemed simple, natural, and effortless. Back in NYC, however, precisely the first moment I was back in my chair, I was halt-ed. Resisted. Dammed. Looking back, the contrast between the two places, between the two states of being, was a gift. I needed the Parisian dream to make me want a new life passion-ately enough to drive me forward. I needed to understand the force it would take to persist against my natural resistance. My wheelchair was literally rubbing the skin off my arms with the effort it took to push it. And I kept pushing it. The omen was unequivocal. Keep going.

I had lived in Kenya at the top of a steep, rain-rutted dirt road up the Menengai Crater. I rolled half of the Camino de Santiago in Spain, kilometres and kilometres a day. I'd rolled all over Europe. Caressed cobblestone, gravel, grass, squelched in mud. Then, while transferring from my chair to the couch, the hundred-pound weight of my body and ten years of adven-ture pressed into the frame and it broke – the entire casing for the front wheel snapped off from the frame of my wheelchair. There was a three-inch gap between the frame and the ground. When I shifted my weight forward to move to the couch, my chair plunged downward and catapulted me out.

I had lived my life so hard the force of me tore metal to shreds.

The same day that my chair broke, I ended up in the ICU with sepsis. A very murdery UTI took me out and refused to succumb to antibiotics. A week later, I was discharged with a semi-permanent IV in my arm, a still-broken wheelchair, and a near-death-fuelled-certainty that it was a great time to get divorced.

CHAPTER TEN

Glitter Helps
New York, New York, U.S., August 2015

The relentless uncertainty of all things took a life-or-death turn. The way my spirit moved through it becomes more tangible with remembering. I survived, I thrived, all things remained uncertain. An uncertainty that became an openness. The rawest awe.

One day my wheel snapped off.

"I can't repair that," the wheelchair mechanic told me.

I hung up, took a nap, called him back. "The Quickie XTR is discontinued," he explained.

I hung up, fell asleep, called him back. "Ma'am, listen," he insisted. "I can't get replacement parts for that."

I hung up, fell asleep. Something wasn't right. My husband was travelling. My dog Foxy and I were on our own.

Shivering and delirious with fever, I called a friend. "I have to go to the hospital, and I don't think I'm coming back tonight. Can you come and walk Foxy for me?"

The next place me and my Quickie XTR went together was to the NYU Langone emergency room where they checked me right into ICU.

I was in ICU, taking selfies in a hospital gown, a pile of wires and tubes pooled at my side. A book in my lap, my thigh exposed. I managed the severity of what was happening with the challenge of making the tedious process of not dying something sexy and entertaining. My friends and I used stage make-up and washable markers and glitter to paint healing symbols on my body.

"The glitter helps," I told the doctor when he came to update me and listen to my heart.

The resident doctor took my care personally right from my first night in the ICU stepdown. He came for his turn at taking my vitals and asking for my medical history and was impressed to learn that I was an aerialist.

"You have good lungs just like we like them. That's a good liver. And that's an amazing tattoo!"

I thanked him and explained that since I was born with no tailbone, I got a ram's head where there was space instead of bone. His eyes gleamed eagerly for the rest of the story. The tuft of hair on the ram's forehead is meant to look like flames, for Aries. Instead of a tailbone, I have fire.

"Do you mind if I do an unnecessary neuro exam?" he asked. I was used to the way my rare condition and unusually paralyzed legs fascinated all levels of doctors.

"Not at all," I said, and I meant it. My relationship to the medical field is complicated. I first learned to love my body by learning how it worked with people who had dedicated their lives to helping me use it. Some tossed careless authority around by imposing limits on how I used it. But these exchanges with doctors instilled a curiosity for my body. It also gave me a language to advocate for my health and well-being. When other girls were learning to judge themselves and forcing their bodies to fit in, I was learning to appreciate my body the way it was. I *relate* to it more than just live in it. I have spent my life tracking its moods and shifts and habits and preferences. When my body gets sick, when it goes slack in some way, I sit with it as though I am sitting with a lover, listening to the rise of my lover's breath to determine if they are comfortable, if they are resting or in distress. I attend to my body. I feel how it needs me. To me, this is what it means to be inhabited. I trust my body, not because it does what I want but because I know it.

Before the resident left, he told me that lungs taking in air separate the first heartbeat slightly but that in most people you can't hear it.

"Something about your physiology makes it more distinct. I think I can actually hear it. It's so cool. It sounds like..." and he mimicked my heart sounds.

I was released after a week, with a port to my heart to allow me to give myself IV antibiotics every day for a couple more weeks.

They said I shouldn't feel it, but when they tested the tube for the first time, I shuddered and asked them what that cool flutter across my chest was. The nurses explained it was the saline flush as it hit my heart. I felt it every time. The instructions they gave me were to firmly pump the syringe and then pause, releasing short but smooth thrusts of fluid deep, deep into me. It was disturbingly sensual. I decided to make a date out of every infusion I gave myself. I wore the lingerie I had just brought back from Paris. Sterile but still seductive.

Laura and I decided to submit a new show for the fall season of Dixon Place while I was still in the hospital.

"Let's say it's our comeback tour... FMBS goes acoustic!" Laura suggested.

We had no idea what that meant, but we knew our shtick well enough to outline the idea of a show. I figured I had enough time to get out of the hospital and regain my strength for a couple aerial pieces. We started writing about my sex appeal and her princess fascination and how both of those things expressed our sense of feminism while I was wearing a hospital gown.

My ex and I had been separated the entire time I lived in New York.

"I will never have sex with you again," I told him when I first relocated. He was still working with the girl with whom he'd had his affair, casually socializing with her and dragging his feet on his plan to switch to another team. I had lost all interest in trying to navigate the psychological and emotional complexity of the situation he created. "I understand if you want a divorce," I said. He didn't want to divorce, so I bought a daybed. I turned the living room into my personal sanctuary with teal velvet chairs and hundreds of books and posters of street art photographed in Paris and Frida Kahlo paintings, and that's where I slept. The bedroom that he occupied started to feel like his Montreal condo: lifeless and bare. We talked every day, shared the details of our lives, went out for dinner together, discussed joint issues, and slept with other people. We were some kind of partners but not a romantic couple. We were two people helping each other resist a tremendous change.

Elliott had been travelling when I was hospitalized, and he arrived home from his trip the day I was released. In order to receive intravenous antibiotics while at home, they inserted what is called a PICC line. It's like an IV, except a long, very thin tube is inserted into your brachial artery in your arm and threaded directly into your heart. The 'port' left on your bicep is where you plug yourself into bags of drugs until your treatment is complete. My arm was so bruised from the PICC procedure that I couldn't push myself. I was in a hospital chair since my three-wheeled death trap was so dangerous they wouldn't release me in it. I had friends come over during the weeks I was on IV antibiotics to take me for walks outside, out for meals, and accompany me to shows. I was weak, and my people rallied.

The first night back to my real life, Laura came. She brought champagne from a party, and we took selfies pretending to attach it to my IV. She pushed me to dinner, and Elliott joined us. He was annoyed when I asked him if he could walk Foxy when we got home, said he was tired from travelling, couldn't I do it? I couldn't, which seemed blatantly obvious to me by the fact that Laura was maneuvering my chair around. This was a level of dependence no one had ever seen from me. All my friends were struck by the strangeness of helping me in this way. Yet Elliott needed it to be pointed out to him. I had to make a case for his help. I had stopped indulging him with earnest explorations of the world through my eyes, the way I had the night the bus driver refused me years before; I had spent a lot of time being frustrated and incredulous instead. Now I was done.

A couple weeks later, after the home nurse removed the IV that went from my arm into my heart and my body was my own again, I asked for a divorce.

There were two reasons I lived in NYC: my husband's job and his work visa. There was one reason I loved it there: Laura von Holt. She was the reason I was on stage, she was the reason I was a sex icon, she was the lifestyle I was living that I loved.

The next day, I joined Laura at rehearsal for our show to tell her.

"I'm getting a divorce," I said bluntly. I needed to say things clear and plain.

Ending things with Elliott was a relief. "You *were* always going to have to do it," he told me when we discussed the specifics, and I understood that I was releasing us both.

But leaving Laura was going to break both of our hearts.

"Once we're divorced, I won't have a visa to live here anymore. I'll have to move."

She gulped, and her eyes got wide. "This is happening? This is happening right now?" She whispered.

"Yes." I waited. She started to cry, and I hugged her. I couldn't grieve yet; I still had to make it happen. Instead, we wrote our goodbyes into the show, which we updated from being a comeback show to the very last show: Flaming Mermaid Broken Star's Farewell Comeback Seduction Tour 2015.

ERIN

There's a reason this is our last show.

LAURA

I totally thought we did that as a marketing gimmick.

ERIN

No. It's real actually. And it's cuz I'm leaving. I'm moving and I'm going away.

LAURA

Wait, is this because I said I was in a relationship with myself?

ERIN

No! I think you are so right for yourself!

LAURA

Thank you!

ERIN

I know I'm leaving you in good hands. I feel okay about that. No. It's not that. I just... have to go.

LAURA

Yeah. I don't get it.

ERIN

Alright. So, you know how I went away on a vision quest...

LAURA

Yeah.

ERIN

Because my imaginary daddy is a viking sea god...

LAURA

Yeah.

ERIN

... you met him that time.

LAURA

Totally.

ERIN

So, there I am on trains in Norway and I'm like, Dad. Imaginary daddy, my life is the best a girl could ever ask for. I live in the greatest city in the world. I have the most famous show anyone has ever seen, my performance partner is so pretty and so smart, and I am a sex icon and everyone wants to have sex with me...

LAURA

SO TRUE!

ERIN

So, why is it that I feel empty inside?

LAURA

I don't know...
    ERIN
... he was like, "It's because you have a dream – to be a European – and you are not living it."
    LAURA
Oh my god.
    ERIN
I know, he's so wise...
    LAURA
Yeah.
    ERIN
... and fireproof.

People often say they wish they had a script for their important moments. A way to slow it down and extract every drop of essence from it, get it right. That's what happens when you write a show about saying goodbye to your best friend in the whole world. We said goodbye in front of a live audience in the form of an aerial routine, set to the music from *Fievel Goes West,* with a giant projection of the moon behind us.

It was hilarious.

But it was not a joke. I was actually leaving New York to go be a European. I recovered something about myself that became clearer and more precise the longer I was married and didn't want to be. It was that long-ago desire to be a European when I grew up. The sensuality, the significance, the lover.

After Paris, I believed in that dream again. The courage to pursue it – which Laura and I wrote into that scene – hadn't come yet.

We performed our goodbye less than a month before I left. By that point, I had made Laura rehearse it a hundred times, and she cried every single time. It was a little sadistic of me, frankly, but every time we fell into the rhythm of the scene, my love for her washed through me like streams through dry river beds, the first trickle of moisture, the first perk of life coming through. I was leaving the love of my life. Not my husband. Her. So we said goodbye over and over and over with the lines of our own script.

CHAPTER ELEVEN

The Death You Don't Die
New York, New York, U.S., October 2015

After my hospitalization, I had my first-ever inclination to ask a doctor about life expectancies for people with conditions like mine. My health was freakishly resilient, but I thought about death all the time. It turned out, my generation is already outliving previous generations. Not institutionalizing us from birth has done wonders for our lifespan. So, the answer is "unspecified." I prefer to think of it as "indefinite," which is both generous and realistic. My sense of my lifespan is the same as before I thought to ask.

I also learned the leading causes of death for a body like mine are sepsis and renal failure. That's a juicy detail. I had just had a septic UTI that distressed my kidneys. Why, there I'd been, almost dying, with no idea I was being statistically relevant.

I still look at the tiny crescent-moon scar on my left bicep from the PICC line they put in to soak my heart in antibiotics. To murder the infection trying to murder me. It's barely any evidence of the fight. If I wear a long-sleeved shirt, the grain of the material pressed into my skin obscures it completely. But I still look for it.

The better evidence is the way I *feel* there is an end, in a penetrating way I didn't before I got sepsis. Different even from the immutability of endedness I felt seeing the casketed body of my little brother at his funeral.

Jesse was my father's son, but we had different mothers. We met when he was five years old and I was twenty-one. I went to North Bay for a visit where his mother told me that, if I wanted, I could be the one to tell him. It was a precious gift. I had always known who my dad was, but he had ignored his paternity. I had aunts and uncles and grandparents because of my relation to this man, but I still had no dad. I cannot explain how that happened. I don't remember how I even knew who he was. I never knew why his family would have me around and raise me among them while he insisted I couldn't be his. Why did they never actively hold him accountable, call him out for lying, shame him for being absent, or believe him and shun me? Instead, I was gossiped about. Which maybe explains why, actually. It was a good story burning through a rural town and I was an easy child to have around, to use as a prop for attention by way of being an unclaimed bastard or adorably disabled. My father had other kids who did not know who I was. But I could tell Jesse. I could acknowledge myself as his sister.

He lived in the house next to my dad's sisters, with whom I was staying, tucked into some Northern Ontario bush off the highway between North Bay and Temiskaming. It was dark in the forest, but the houses gave enough light between them to light our footing. We trudged over the grass and I told him.

"Jesse, do you know that I am your sister? Brian is my dad, too."

He got shy, tucking his chin into the collar of his coat, maybe even sucking it into his mouth. I am tempted to say that I could see his freckles in the glow of the house lights, but I don't know if I could – that's just how I always picture his face. The bridge of his nose and cheekbones smattered in freckles.

"Is it true?" He asked me and asked his mother again when we got to his house.

Once he let himself believe it, he was excited. The next time I visited, it was for our Grampy's funeral. During the reception, in the basement of the church I had grown up going to, Jesse bounced around singing. "My sister, Erin. My sister, Erin."

Another daughter of Brian's was sitting across the table from me. She narrowed her sixteen-year-old eyes. Sixteen was too old to be learning about a half-sister, and it was too terrible to find out indirectly at our shared grandfather's funeral. Both of our lives were filled with this kind of tragic absurdity. If we had anything else in common, it was the unflinching look in her eyes and the lack of emotion in her voice.

"Jesse's mom doesn't have a daughter, does she?" she asked me, knowing the answer. I shook my head, holding eye contact.

"You're... Brian's?" She glanced to her mother who was sitting at the end of the same table, who nodded. Her mother didn't deny it but wasn't eager to explain it either.

The next funeral I attended was Jesse's. He died when he was sixteen years old in a snowmobiling accident while I was in New York waiting to hear news of our ailing father. Who, instead of dying himself, was released from the hospital in time to attend the funeral of his son.

"Corinne told me about you, with your dad and stuff," a friend of Jesse's mom said to me in the sitting room of the funeral parlour at Jesse's wake. "How are you not bitter?" she asked with a touch of admiration. In that moment, my lack of anger seemed like a red flag to me, not a virtue. I had no answer for her.

During the funeral, I headed outside to sip fresh air and ended up on the sidewalk with Brian. He leaned against his cane with a frailty caused by layers of heartbreak – grief and literal heart failure.

"Sorry I forgot to put your name with the siblings in Jesse's obituary." It was the closest he had ever come to acknowledging his paternity.

And now, after my brush with sepsis, I have felt the threshold of death with my own heartbeats.

When my bladder wreaks a spasm or I have a freak overnight fever, I automatically plan to have very little time left. It's not a sentimental thing. Just a calm scroll through what I'd need to do in the event it was happening again.

Brushes with death are uncanny. The death you don't die is not like actually dying. I am unequivocally alive. Jesse is very dead. An astonishing difference between people. And yet, my un-died death seems reluctant to move on. It's on my mind a lot. I think it wants to be friends. I'm okay with that. Mortality isn't as dreadful company as we're led to believe. I'm not friends with Jesse's death, though. That death is a sociopath and a thief.

One of the most powerful conversations I have ever had was on a restaurant patio in Toronto with the same friend who inspired me to visit Ottawa. He became a doctor, specifically an infectious disease specialist, and an ICU doctor. He essentially manages people's deaths for a living. We were having lunch on a sunny afternoon months after my health was well in the clear again.

"They gave me a form to fill out. You know, who gets to make medical decisions when I stop being able to give consent to stuff. I just put it in a drawer without filling it out," I babbled. I affected a casual, unconcerned air, but I couldn't hold the act for long. I may have just whispered the next part. "If it happens again, could I put your name?" I went nowhere near eye contact.

"Yes," he said, immediately shouldering the weight of my request. "How would you want me to handle it?" he asked, adjusting his cutlery into, out of, then back into symmetry.

"Fight until it wasn't worth winning," I said firmly, stroking the stem of my wine glass.

"That's what I figured you'd want."

And that was it.

I hope he never has to be there for me in this way, but it gave me such tremendous peace to know that I have him to attend to me if I need it. As an expert in infections that intend to kill me and the whole intensive care circumstances in which I'd likely die, it's like he spent a bajillion years training himself to know how to fight, precisely, for me. Just in case. As a long-standing best friend who knows my love of a dramatic and beautiful narrative above all else, as well as countless other details of me that matter, he would know when it wasn't worth winning anymore.

And how to tell the story after.

I know I am in spectacular hands, even in the worst possible circumstances. I *feel* it. It's better than certainty.

"If you could choose, how would you want to die?" my friend asked me another time, during one of our late-night conversations when his kids were in bed so we could say stuff like that. I listed off diseases I thought would be as painless as

– but more romantic than – death by bladder, and he ruined my fantasies of peaceful ends, refuting each with medical facts.

"Fine! I want to get eaten by jungle leopards!" I exclaimed, half-exasperated, half-laughing. I was thinking I'm glad it's not up to me.

"Don't you want to leave behind a beautiful corpse?" he parried.

I laughed, but something about the one-liner took me out of the moment. I remembered the corpse of my baby brother. In vivid detail. Trailing the top of my finger along his wrist bone. His skin felt artificial. I wanted to touch him more firmly, but I was worried the makeup would rub off or something grotesque would happen. I sat on the couch next to his open coffin for hours instead. It was both helpful and horrifying.

The October during my divorce mediation, I took my dog Foxy to the Tompson Square dog park in the East Village. There was a new guy among all the regulars. He wore a knit scarf and had a ridiculous wiener dog named Montell.

"This is how we do it!" I sang. He was impressed because I got the right Montell.

"Most people ask why I named my dog after a TV show host."

I rolled my eyes and pointed to Montell wiggling by. "He's clearly a lower-case g."

We liked the same kind of jokes. Sharp ones. The kind that mean you can say true things too soon to a stranger because you can say them funny. You can observe each other dispassionately and therefore much more closely. It's a social contract where, if you can keep the banter going, you agree to share the effort of balancing between snark and sincerity. It's thrilling. More so when the person is so new to you that you can't rely on historical context to determine their intent or how hard you can push. All you have is a shared belief in the mysterious and intimate good will you have for each other. I can't dance in a standing-up way – body to body, intensity swelling between me and another from proximity – but I can dance like this.

We teased each other, and I mentioned I was in the middle of a divorce and I had no idea where I would live next.

"I thought Berlin might be fun," I said. "But it wasn't. Not sexy enough. I hear Spain is sexier." I admitted I was nervous about the transition I was about to go through in which, exactly as I had always wanted, I had to decide everything. I couldn't explain why I was so afraid, so I was flip about it. I riffed back and forth on the different kinds of lives I might live when my life was my own again. In the lulls, I brooded.

"Hey," he said, getting me to look at him and realize he meant it. "I'm happy for you." He took my number and left.

A few days later I got a text: Why are you sitting on the loser bench?

I looked up and saw him sitting on the other side of the dog park. I rolled over and sat next to him. I liked our style – insulting each other in greeting.

"I'm on my way to California," he said. "My aunt's funeral."

"I'm so sorry," I said and then held back, waited as he gathered himself to say more.

"She committed suicide." He paused again, checking to see if this was the kind of conversation our fresh connection could handle. It could.

"She talked all the time about feeling trapped in her marriage. You know, at family gatherings and stuff. We all kind of... well, anyway I thought she was just letting off steam. People feel trapped in marriages sometimes... that's normal, right?

They don't kill themselves over it. If she had wanted to leave, we would have helped her. I had no idea it could feel so impossible that suicide would be a real alternative..." He was looking out at the dogs playing, visibly aching with helplessness. Then he turned to me. "I think you're saving your own life right now, Erin. That's why I was happy when you told me you were getting a divorce. I don't think it's easy. I know you're scared, but I really believe you'll be okay."

I never heard from him again. I didn't need to. By that time, I knew what it was like to be pulled back into life. It was disorienting and anticlimactic, more of a steady trudge of not slipping away than a dramatic reanimation.

In October, I still had bruises on my arm from the PICC line. I still had a strange weariness inside of me. I had been sick two months before, but now I was better. I was suspicious of myself for feeling weary.

One day, a dog park acquaintance who had heard about my health scare stopped to check in with me as I passed on the sidewalk.

"How are you?" she asked, and I shrugged and squinted, looking for words.

"You're still feeling... weird, then." Weird wasn't the right word either, but she said it with so much understanding. "I have Lyme disease," she continued. A condition whose treatment also involves PICC lines and massive doses of antibiotics and trying not to die. "It's like, the antibiotics or something. They wipe you out. They make you better, but then you're... hollow. It takes a while to feel like yourself again."

I was as suspicious of feeling weary about my divorce as I was feeling weary about my health. I was being unkind toward my pain. I assumed if something had happened, was handled, and everything was fine, I should be neutral and grateful. I hadn't connected the dying my body had faced from sepsis with the dying my spirit was fighting its way out of with divorce. Not until a guy with a dog named after an R&B singer from the '90s appeared in my life and made it for me. Once I had the connection, I heard what both of these friends were offering me.

Everything in my life edged up against death, and near-deaths leave marks. Divorce, sepsis, wheelchairs that don't work and take six months to replace. If all I could do now was wait for things to stop feeling scary and hollow, I might as well assume whatever time it took – the lack of rush into and out of this all-encompassing transformation – was itself a kindness.

As a Canadian living in NYC on a dependent's visa, a divorce meant being catapulted from my home. My body was wrecked. My chair was wrecked. My life was wrecked. Everything had plunged downward and catapulted me out. I was reeling and lost and wounded everywhere.

My divorce was impeccably amicable. We had four meetings with a mediation lawyer. One month in total. I wanted to feel safe, mainly financially. He wanted to feel smart, also mainly financially. We checked in often; we made sure we each were getting what we needed from the process. We took each other out for snacks and treats after meetings. We were never right for each other in the way I needed and wanted to be with someone. But we were right for each other when it came time to end it.

And I was still wiped out by panic, and disoriented. The divorce papers were signed. I was on a train back to Canada. There were mere days between events. One day, the world was known. The next day I was hollow. I couldn't eat. I slept and cried. My brain made no sense and I huddled in the spare rooms and couches of friends all over the world. Friends who didn't make me account for myself. Who had no doubt I would be fine but didn't rush me to be sure of that before my grief was complete. Friends who knew I was grieving in the first place, when I thought I was just trying to plan a regular life and couldn't figure out why I couldn't figure anything out – they knew it was grief.

I wanted to live in Europe, but I didn't know what country or what I would do there. I had the vague idea I was still an aerialist. That part of me was intact. So, I looked for places where I could train. A friend had acquired an artist visa to live in Berlin, there were circus spaces there. But I had visited Berlin while the divorce was unfolding, and it didn't click. Instead, I had a series of other places to visit and no plan. I stayed with a circus friend in Edinburgh, I took a workshop with an aerial rope coach at the circus in Barcelona, but first, I spent Christmas in Hawai'i with Laura's family.

We split time between a ranch house in the mountains with a green so vivid and endless, and a beach house with lava rocks instead of beach sand and guest mumus to wear for lounging. It was breeding season for humpback whales and, at night, I could hear them exhale seawater breaths. I rested. I was around people who were together and rooted, and that was how I remembered to be together and rooted. I healed.

Laura drove me through tropical rain to a volcano hissing in the downpour. I poured gin in offering to the most fiery goddess who had just gushed lava straight through a small town, completely destroying it and yet leaving the freshest earth on the planet. I thought about how violent creating life is. When a volcano spits out molten lava, it doesn't just flow over land, it devours it. Entire towns, neighbourhoods, distinct geographical features, all succumb entirely to the onslaught of earth in its molten form. I had seen images of volcanic eruptions, the gash in the earth, exposing its blood, its life force. The rivers of lava sputtering and churning. I was expecting adrenaline and drama.

Laura and I drove to a viewing site that had been coordinated by volunteers for the local children, whose entire town had been split in half by a river of liquid fire. Where the lava flows, it stays, the topography of their lives irrevocably altered. The town felt that being able to see the lava for themselves would help the children grieve, give context to the sudden and massive change, perhaps even appreciate the nature of the power of their home. So they set up a viewing station where children could bus in, talk with volunteers, learn about lava, see the edges of new earth where the lava had finally cooled and gone still. Flowers had been tossed (or placed) over the orange safety fence at the edge of the smooth, black rock where it overlapped on the grey, manmade tarmac.

In this way, the Big Island of Hawai'i is literally growing. But the fresh earth, the new lava, will take decades or more before it turns to soil. When it's fresh, it's useless. My life had erupted like a volcano. From an actual volcano, I learned that it takes time to be fertile, and I was with Laura when I learned it.

In January of 2015, I got my new chair. A Tilite Aero Z titanium frame with the exact same measurements as my previous chair. I moved all my stuff and the broken chair from my ex's apartment into my mom's basement, got a one-year residency visa, and then I moved to Spain.

PART TWO

IMPOSSIBLE THINGS

It's impossible to tell what the risk will yield. Little
coin toss. Is it a loss... or a win? *Little eye, unblinking.*
Little mole on the skin. Could be malignant, could be
benign. Little navel. Little nostril. Little knot in the
wood of longing.

—RISK: AN ACCOUNTING
BRENDA MILLER AND JULIE MARIE WADE

CHAPTER TWELVE

The Unknown Factor
Zermatt, Switzerland, June 2016

The best part of moving to Spain was how close it was to the rest of Europe. Several times a month, whenever the whim struck me, I travelled. First I sailed the fjords from Bergen to Kirkenes, deep into the Arctic Circle in the middle of winter to hunt Northern Lights. I wrote so much about that trip that I turned it into a magazine for my friends and family to purchase.

Then I went to Paris for the third time. It was early spring and I was full of ease and joy. I knew my way around so well, I had friends to visit. I was at home in Paris as I had always dreamed.

Then, one of the friends I had made at sea in Norway and I decided to do a two-week road trip together in the Alps. He could drive, and loved to. I could *not* drive, but wanted to go to the kind of places you could only access by car. That was how, in July of 2016, I was in Zermatt having my first ever paragliding experience.

But first I have to tell you about the Valais sheep.

The thing I most wanted from my road trip in the Alps was to make friends with some alpine cows. The tonk tonk of their bells in the distance gave me peaceful feelings, and I was sure we were meant to bond. But I was wrong and the cows were not interested. I saw many in the stretch we drove from Salzburg, through South Tyrol in Italy, back through Austria and then Switzerland. But there was no friendship. And I had come to accept it.

On the way we stayed in Zermatt, a fancy and populated break from our usual isolated choices because friends of ours, a Swiss couple we met on the same Norwegian cruise, would be there. Zermatt is a car-free mountain resort nestled in the Swiss Alps, accessible only by train, known most famously for the iconic Matterhorn that presides over the town. While there, I learned there was a special herd of traditional sheep up in the mountains with curly black fur on their noses and knees and tourists could go visit them – after an intrepid, Swiss-mountain hike, of course.

As usual, I was not deterred.

One night, my group of friends headed to a restaurant that turned out to be owned by the family who also owned the sheep. We asked the waitress about the excursion and promptly the patriarch of the sheep himself towered, grave-faced, over our table to hear our petition: Could I and my wheelchair visit the herd?

The word? Meet here tomorrow morning.

The next morning there was a small group gathered. An equally tall but more dimpled member of the sheep dynasty bounced toward us to explain which gondolas we'd be taking to get to the top.

The cable car operators stopped the line when it was my turn to roll on and our group of four piled in and I got giddy for sheep.

While everyone assembled at the top and prepared to hike, a lanky man appeared suddenly and reached out his hand, saying, 'Hi! I'm Hubert, I will be driving your jeep!'

Ah! So *that's* how we would make this work.

I climbed in and Hubert loaded my chair into the back and we left the hikers in our dust!

He told me how hard it can be to find the herd who climb up into the rocks and look like patches of snow. He told me how awed he was with the patriarch's sheep dog.

"I was out there trying to eat my lunch and the dog rounded all the sheep up in a huddle and drove them to me until I had no space. So, I just moved away, but he knows his job so well – he rounded them all up again and herded them over to me."

"So, are you a shepherd?" I asked.

"No, I'm the chef," he laughed. "I cook the sheep."

As we drove, Hurbert slowed for each person we passed, in case they needed help. Sometimes to encourage them to keep going. Always to toss a greeting.

"Is that them?" I squinted at a speck in the distance. I had heard a friendly bell tonk faintly. "You have incredible senses," he said, "but no. I have a trick if we can't find them." He showed me a GPS tracker.

In the end, we found them without the GPS, huddling and doing not much else up above the Stafelalp. And they knew the truck.

"Are you frightened?" Hubert asked as they began to gather. "They're very gentle. But they will come to us now – all together. They know we have food."

I didn't answer, I was already out the door and sitting on the ledge of the jeep waiting for my chair as the herd ambled toward us.

"They like shade," Hubert explained as I hopped into my chair. Immediately I could go nowhere as I was entirely surrounded. Heads bowed toward the one small square of shade cast under my seat.

"They can be a little skittish if you touch them," Hubert warned. So I reached tentatively to one that was licking the fabric of my seat cushion. She didn't flinch, so I wrapped my hand around her horn and pushed. She pushed back and licked me and then went back to licking my seat. I pushed my hand into the tufts of springy hair on the nearest heads, nudging those who nudged me.

The ones who got to me first started to press their woolly bodies into my metal frame, and the rest of the herd pressed into them, and more into that layer, five or six rows deep.

"I can feel them breathing!" I gasped. The herd breathed as a collective. Their inhaling and exhaling rocked me smoothly. A motion I could feel exquisitely – particularly through my unbraked wheels. "I'm inside the herd," I said. "I'm..."

Hubert had been busy preparing snacks and wine for the rest of the group, getting feed ready for the sheep. He looked at me with the calm of totally getting it. "It's so good that you can let it feed you. Most people just look at this and take a photo and say, 'Oh, that's wonderful,' and pass by."

We had a while before the group, and my friends, joined. Hubert enticed the herd away from me with food and I moved into the sun. He poured me some wine and the herd surrounded me again. I sipped. And we breathed. And I memorized the feel of that rocking into my bones.

Eventually, the rest of the group arrived. They took photos with the herd, drank some wine, and then we headed off to the mountain outpost of the family restaurant where Hubert would change into chef's clothes and make us all (not-sheep-based) lunch.

As we drove, Hubert pointed to a tiny spot of colour floating in the sky–a parachute with a person attached.

He asked, "Do you plan on doing that while you're here?"

"What is that?" I asked.

"It's paragliding."

"You can just paraglide? Like, I can do that?"

It had never occurred to me to be interested in paragliding. I assumed it took a lot of specialized, expensive, hard-to-access training and practice to get to the point where you could turn yourself into a tiny speck of colour in a vast sky. Also, I happen to be afraid of heights. I don't know what made Hubie suggest it, maybe he was teasing me, maybe he sensed something. But, if you could simply want to, and then *do* it, I wanted to. I wanted to be someone who could fly. I didn't even know how it worked. But, in my mind, I had already traded places with the speck in the sky. Hubert and the rest were still rumbling around the Matterhorn in a jeep looking for a herd of rare and protected sheep, and I was soaring far above.

I often learn about a place or an activity and am flooded with longing for it and, with no understanding of the logistics or how my limits will change them, I show up to try. But there are many adventurous, daredevil things that don't appeal to me. Skydiving. Bungee jumping, because it is easy for me to picture myself doing it. Without meaningful unknown factors, it is just raw thrill. I need more. I need a process. I need to *want* to do something but not know *how* I will do it.

How will I get in the air? How will I land?

If I find a compelling adventure and answer the questions on the first try, I will often abandon the pursuit. If it proves impossible to adapt without so much facilitation that I become a passenger in the experience, I abandon it. The best things for me have a continuously unfolding layer of uncertainty. The question of "how" keeps refreshing. I'm after inexhaustible wonderment – wonderment for my body, for the process, for the results. When wonderment is present, it becomes a more powerful motivation than even a primal fear of heights can deter.

When my learning requires adaptations that take us outside the experience of whatever expert is helping me, it heightens the appeal of taming the unknown. The unknown thing – it isn't just the sky and the mountains, it isn't the activity and my wheelchair colliding. The unknown factor is me. Back in the jeep, Hubert just shrugged. "Oh, yeah, no problem. They have an office in town where they take anyone up to experience it. You should sign up!"

He explained that in a tandem flight the passenger is strapped to the pilot and is somewhat incidental to the entire thing. They could be there, or not be there, the pilot still flies. So "anyone" can be a passenger on a tandem flight in the same way that "anyone" can be a passenger on a bus. Still it is also true that "anyone" doesn't always include people with disabilities. Sometimes there are sound reasons, and sometimes they just won't let you on the bus. I didn't typically like being incidental to anything, but I was a tourist in a tourist town that did tourist paragliding flights in view of the Matterhorn, and it sounded fun. If they would take me, I would try it.

"I am going to sign up!" I had an intuition that paragliding was already mine, and once we returned to town, I headed straight to the tour company office run by Australian paragliding pilots.

It was a last-minute attempt to try a popular activity on my last day in town, but the pilots were enthusiastic about making it happen.

I am drawn to people who see an obstacle and consider it a source of fun. Who see potential. Those people see me in my wheelchair and take me seriously when I say I'd like to do something. They think, "Yeah, we could figure this out." Those people are rare and marvellous treasures. It seemed paragliding pilots were those kind of people.

"If it was up to me," said one of the pilots, with a heavy Australian accent that made even his vowels sound adventurous, "I would just strap you into the chair and attach the whole thing to the harness." He wasn't joking, and his voice revealed the gleam of a rogue idea. There wasn't enough time to work out the safety factors of attaching a harness to a wheelchair, but there were other logistics to chew on to keep him thrilled.

Pursuing autonomy while disabled is like being the honey badger from the viral YouTube video "Honey Badger Houdini." It's the story of a honey badger named Stoffel who keeps escaping from his pen in a South African animal sanctuary. After the honey badger climbed a tree and bent the branch to the wall to escape, the caretaker trimmed the branches of all the trees in the enclosure. When the honey badger urinated on the dirt to make mud that he could pack up against the cement wall and climb out, the caretaker installed a mesh overhang. The honey badger outsmarted the caretaker every single time. It would be easy to assume the honey badger wanted freedom in the wilderness, but one night, he smashes the window of the caretaker's house, who wakes up to hear Stoffel scratching at his bedroom door. "Every time I devised some plan it was like a game for him to work out, how could he get over this," the caretaker surmises in the video. A game in which the honey badger seriously risked being mauled by the sanctuary's resident lion – again.

I felt that way about adventure and possibly life in general. It was a game to work out how to get out of the enclosures built around me, over the obstacles set in my way. Lions, beware of me.

In North Bay, I went to kindergarten and primary school at Marshall Park. The principal of the school called my mother one morning to tell her that the school would be having a massive gym exercise.

"Everyone will be running around, and we're worried that Erin might get hurt," he told her.

When she tells me the story now, she points out how, at that point, I wore leg braces up to my hips. I was covered in metal and plastic and used to falling, so if anyone was likely to get hurt, it was some other kid.

I wanted to play Cinderella in the school play, I wanted to do gymnastics with the other students. I loved to act and tumble. When I played alone, I was either in character or tossing my body around. I felt free, my whole being engaged in activity. But when I would do this on the playground at school, they would call my mother, fretting, "Erin is on the monkey bars. What should we do?"

"Did she fall?" my mother would ask.

"Well, no," they admitted, "but she's hanging upside down."

I couldn't squeeze my legs toward my butt the way other kids did to keep their legs hooked over the bar without holding on. Instead, I used my leg braces, thick plastic that came up to just under my knee, by wedging the bar between the lip of my braces and the back of my knee and resting my ankles under the next bar over. The weight of my body – gravity – locked me in place.

"Call me when there's blood," my mother would say, dismissively.

I was doing what kids were supposed to do – playing on equipment that had been built in the playground to be played on by kids. But I was not supposed to do that. The refrain of school administration was that their concern was for my well-being, but I was happy and doing what I wanted and what I could. So who was this concern *really* for?

My mother always defended me. But she wasn't prepared for the direct resistance it required to get into the places I wanted to go and to be part of what I wanted to join. The barriers were relentless; "no" was not only common but inevitable. She let me do what I wanted to do, but she preferred following rules to breaking them. I got to do the fighting, the confronting, the part where I showed up anyway, over and over, put myself on the line, took the hit. I had the desire and the stamina for it. It was like a game to me. But it was an exhausting game, and I rested from the effort in the company of trees. I loved it when it was just the woods and me and how trees smell and the way the light filters through needles, leaves, and branches. I settle deeply into myself when I am with trees.

North Bay, the town in which I was born, where my kindergarten was, is settled on the Canadian Shield, a 4,790,000-square-kilometre terrain shaped like a U, in which

the geological core of the North American continent is exposed – the first piece of land pushed up above the sea. My
favourite game as a kid was to "play house," which, for me,
meant crawling across three-billion-year-old rocks that had
once been the tallest mountains on the planet, but which were
now gentle hills covered in moss and lichen. When I was "hidden" by spruce trees and felt far away and very alone, I would
make "tea" from leaves and talk to my own mind out loud.
When we moved from North Bay to London, Ontario, I ex-
changed the rocks for the ravine that bordered our housing
complex. It seemed massive when I was nine, but the next
road over was visible through the trees in most parts. I would
scramble down, cross the tiny stream, and try to feel alone.
I was allowed to be whatever and whoever *I* was, with no resistance – but only when I was alone.

At some point in the midst of all my refusing to sit safely
and not play, the principal of my first primary school told my
mother, "Someday, someone is going to have to tell her she's
disabled."

"I have spent her whole life telling her she isn't," my mother
replied.

He didn't have to worry. Someone would. *Everyone* would.
I would be reminded of my proper place over and again, sent
back to whatever "pen" the disabled people were kept "safe" in.

And I would break out again and again. I was breaking out
when I was in Zermatt, asking if I could paraglide.

To get to Rothorn, the peak from which we would launch,
we would have to ride a gondola up the mountain. If I took
my wheelchair up with me, it would still be up there when I
landed. So, the Australian pilots borrowed a wheelchair so they
could leave mine at the landing spot. That was how I learned

that the pilot's control of the glider is precise enough that he can choose where he and his passenger land in advance – not at all like the random floating I had imagined.

On the gondola they played songs about flying to get into the mood. At the station, they rolled me out in the borrowed wheelchair and showed me the grassy slope we still had to get down to get to the launch site. It was too steep to safely wheel down, so we waited a moment, considering whether it was better for me to scramble on my hands and knees or strap into the harness I would fly in and let a couple pilots carry it between them. I preferred to get there on my own if I could, so we did both. I scrambled until I got tired, then they strapped me into the harness and hauled me to the edge.

We had to wait for a flyable wind so, for a while, we just sat there. The guys scanned for rare and protected edelweiss. When they found some, they carefully placed stones around so people would be more likely to see it and not trample the delicate flower.

I was terrified as we waited for a "good breeze"; I had no idea how to identify a good breeze for flying. And where we waited, there was nothing but edge. Nothing was tethering me to the ground. There was no plan B. There was just run, edge… open sky. My heart thrummed in my throat while the pilots sang and waited with ease.

And then there was some imperceptible shift in the wind, and they were suddenly ready. I had been sitting in the harness and now they connected me to the glider. Carabiners clipped against metal hooks, pilot hands squeezed and tugged at all the straps and clamps, testing that everything was secure. My pilot's name was Phil, and he stood close behind me, connected to the same glider. Two other pilots, not attached to anything, grabbed the harness I was in and lifted, just like they had done to haul me down the slope. Phil pulled the lines attached to the wing and it rose above us. The harness pulled tight near my face, pressing into my shoulder, my body jostled by his legs from behind and the jerking of the pilots on either side as the group ran toward the edge. "I got it! Thanks, guys!" Phil called, and the hands released us, the pilots on the ground stumbling to slow down.

The second I was airborne, the harness under me was pulled taut by the gilder above. I was cradled in the tension between harness and glider. I expected to feel a sudden ungrounding, like in a dream about falling, maybe slower but just as full of that sickening sense of unending void. But my weight in the harness was solid.

Buddhist Chögyam Trungpa has said about consciousness and meditation, "The bad news is you're falling through the air, nothing to hang on to, no parachute. The good news is, there is no ground."

Facing a risk triggers fear, and in reaction we are often afraid of the right thing, but for the wrong reason. I imagine the venerable Chögyam meant that we have the exact opposite reaction to our fear than the one that will liberate us. We cement our fears in place and cling to them like ledges, tell ourselves it's security as we grasp and tense at life and time as it passes the way clouds move through the sky. In formations, bringing weather, impermanently. We flinch at the shadows life casts on us without realizing that what we are doing is worse than the impact we fear.

Courage isn't having no fear, it is knowing the true nature of what you fear. You can only learn this by looking right at it. I have always thought that surrender was more about letting yourself really look at fear, at pain, at yourself, than it was about passively letting anything happen to you or not caring how it works out. The first step to taking a risk is to simply open your eyes and look.

"Take the brakes," Phil said. A paraglider is controlled by applying various amounts of pressure to a set of lines called "the brake lines." A nylon cord with a handle leads to a branching of several more nylon cords that are attached equidistantly across different points of the glider. When pulled evenly, it uniformly changes the shape of the glider, which slows it down and acts as steering. Phil helped me loop my hands in the controls. "Press one of your hands down," he instructed. I pressed tenderly, too gently, he pushed his hand on top of mine to show how much pressure I needed and released his hand. "A bit more," he encouraged and I applied more force. The glider turned in the direction of my pressing hand. It responded! I could feel, through the tension on the lines between my hands and the fabric of the glider, the very shape and movement of the air.

"You can control it!" I squealed. Euphoria coursed through me, indistinguishable from terror, which I also felt.

Once I could breathe normally, I was grilling Phil: "Could I learn this? Like, not just fly with someone like this, but actually on my own? How would I get myself off the mountain? How do people learn it? Where would I do it?"

"Oh, there are schools that teach it," he answered, as nonchalantly as if I was inquiring where to learn to read. "There are schools in Spain, for sure. You'll probably need help getting in the air, but you could totally fly on your own. You need to get into paragliding." We swooped around the Matterhorn for another twenty minutes. Phil told me about the theory that birds can see temperature changes in the air, and he pointed out the spot he had had a mid-mountain breakfast with another pilot that morning. We were having a friendly conversation more than 3,300 metres above the ground.

We landed at the exact spot where my chair was waiting for me. I tucked my legs into the harness and we landed – more like sat – very gently on our butts. I was giggling and speech-less. But I didn't need words; Phil and the pilots on the ground knew exactly how I felt. My body was still swooping, still above the Alps. I beamed wordlessly at anyone who asked if I had en-joyed it. I flopped back against Phil, trying to hold myself up. He wrapped his arms around me in celebration and kissed the top of my helmet.

Paragliding was not just flight, it was love.

CHAPTER THIRTEEN

"Take" Me
Algodonales, Spain, November 2016

The first thing I did when I got back to Spain from Switzerland was look up paragliding schools. Goal: autonomous solo flight. But I didn't say that when I emailed José at Zero Gravity Paragliding. Instead, I asked if it was possible to get some training and more flight experience. "I can get around pretty good in mountains," I promised. I was hedging, courting this opportunity. But I was also preparing for him to turn me down.

But José didn't turn me down. He said, "Sure. No problem," then found me the only accessible room in Algodonales, tracked down an adapted harness, and trained himself in it for a few days before I arrived.

My first course with Zero Gravity Paragliding school in Andalucía was in November of 2016. The first time I met the other pilots on my course was in a gas-leaking, dust-encrusted, over-sized van filled with paragliding students and our instructors as it bounced up the side of a mountain. I was wearing huge, dark sunglasses. I wore them whenever I wanted to feel protected in a crowd, as a woman, in a wheelchair. Sunglasses couldn't cover the conspicuous vulnerability of a wheelchair, but they did give me an unapproachable quality, and that bought me time to observe the men who would be in my company for the next week.

I was a brand-new student. Another pilot, a cute guy from Costa Rica named Mau, had three previous weeks of paragliding instruction from José. Mau and José were sitting behind me falling into a familiar rapport that relied heavily on exchanging jokes. I was learning Spanish and liked practising, so I leaned over the back of my seat and listened in, translating José's joke to myself.

A soldier new to a base in the desert asks what the guys do when they want to have sex.

"Oh we just 'take' a camel," his commanding officer tells him.

After much resisting, the soldier eventually and very desperately gives in and tries to have sex with one of the camels. He gets pretty beat up by camel hooves in the process.

He drags his battered body back to base, his face bruised and bloodied.

"Oh my god! What happened?" His commanding officer asks.

"I tried to fuck one of the camels!"

"What? Why?"

"You said that's what you do for sex around here."

"No, I said we take the camels... into town... where the brothel is!"

The joke is how I learned that *coger* – "to take" – has entirely different connotations in Latin America than it does in Spain.

"Every time they ask me to 'take' my glider or yell for someone to 'take' the van, it cracks me up," Mau said, chuckling.

I laughed too. And I took off my huge, dark sunglasses.

José had done some research and found a pilot in another region in Spain who was also paralyzed. He had devised a harness for himself and rented it to José for the week that I was learning. Before I arrived, José took test flights in it so he would know what it was like for me, how it would be different than with his other students. The harness was a styrofoam rectangle box covered in hot pink and blue canvas. The shoulder straps of a regular harness were sewn right into the canvas, and the styrofoam walls came up under my armpits. The canvas zipped up to my chest. It had tiny wheels at the back end for towing. It looked like a race car and felt like a coffin. It worked in that I needed something to keep my legs protected while taking off and landing, but my torso was completely encased, restricting my range of motion.

Whenever someone wandered over to comment on how amazing it was – the harness and the disabled student flying in it – José would deflect them, saying, "This is nothing new." The guy José rented the gear from was paralyzed, and he had made it for himself so he could fly solo. So, we knew there was at least one other person adapting paragliding. But it was new to us. José had never had a disabled student before, and I had all of twenty minutes of previous flight experience.

"I'm *doing* nothing different," José would say to me about what I was learning and how I was doing. And I could see for myself that was true. I am very strict with myself about earning a sense of accomplishment. I didn't just want to fly, which I could do in tandem, I wanted to *learn* how to control my wing, to *know* what I was doing, to *feel* a command of my choices and a connection to their consequences. I wanted clarity, and autonomy, and I was trying to build a sense of myself as a pilot out of an honest assessment. But I had so many instructors involved in my takeoff I was having a very hard time gauging how much my own skill was contributing. So José started to point out how it was similar, between me and other pilots, which allowed me to consider how it was different and what I could improve.

Watching other new pilots take off, one instructor would stand near the pilot, and another would stand in the flight path, facing the pilot to see how straight their wing was, instructing them on their arm placement moment by moment. Now and then the instructors would tug the lines on a student's glider to correct the wing, or pull and push the pilot into a better position mid-launch.

It was pretty standard to toss pilots off mountains when they needed a hand.

On the first day of the course, Mau carried me out of the roughly ploughed sunflower field where I had landed, about a hundred and fifty metres away, without showing a single sign of strain. Normally people huff and pant and I sag in the space between their arms, until my neck aches from pressing against their arm and I ask them to bounce me up higher. Each footfall jolts me. But I couldn't feel Mau's steps. Something in the way he walked was softer, more like the smooth movement of wheels I'm used to. Mau held me firm, my face so close to his face that I had to bend and tilt my head to tuck my cheek against his neck.

"When I carry my future husband or wife over the threshold, I will think of you," he said that first day in the field.

Then you better be future marrying me, I had thought to myself.

Being carried presents a frustrating, one-sided intimacy I would normally avoid. No matter how flirty and playful we made it, the reality is that being carried put him in control of my safety, my bodily autonomy, my comfort. I could know someone for years and never be that dependent on them. In fact, I don't remember Elliott carrying me once. He wasn't the type. And I wouldn't have let him. But when Mau carried me, it felt good.

Later, when José suggested I just let him carry me across the road from the van to the bar so they wouldn't have to unload my chair, Mau hip-checked him out of the way. "Wouldn't you rather I carry you?" he grinned, a little lopsided, his body so tall and warm, the entire risk of him, all that charm. *Yes, I very much would.*

After that, Mau made a point of carrying me. When the situation called for it, and frequently when it was unnecessary. I assumed he liked holding me as much as I liked to be in his arms, but he never explicitly said this, he just found pointless reasons to press me into his chest, wearing his cologne when he learned I liked the scent of it.

He also made a point of meeting most of my random desires that week. He brought me sandwiches with hearts drawn on the plastic wrap, fetched me grapes and a packet of painkillers, split dessert with me every night, and took photos of me for my ongoing documentation of my life as a sex icon.

A flirtatious tension pulsed between us. There was something stirring that drew me irresistibly closer, and something frivolous about the encounters that kept me cautious. I didn't want a fling, and I could tell Mau was just passing through.

In the end, my wheelchair made almost no difference in learning to paraglide except that everyone else flew in standard black harnesses and I flew in a hot pink race car. When other pilots built a wall by inflating their glider slightly to make sure it was evenly distributed and facing directly into the wind, I built a wall of babes, who fanned out in front of me and inflated and controlled my glider for me, holding me safely in place until it was time to let me fly.

This meant that the only obstacle left was my own anxiety.

"You're gonna do a solo flight this week, right?" Mau urged me one night. We were sitting in the back of the van, the entire group driving me home to my villa just outside town after dinner. He'd had his first solo flight on his third day of lessons. It might have been my third day when he brought it up.

I sighed. "I don't think I'm going to make it. I'm still so nervous in the air, and that's with José right there." The winds had been rough and the sky bumpy for days. "I'm preparing myself in case it doesn't happen."

A couple days into the course, while I sat in the shade of the van waiting to fly, Mau bounced up to me and said, "Erin! Let's make a paragliding movie!"

"An action film!" I grinned.

"Exactly!," he said, and tucked into the van beside me.

There's a lot of waiting in paragliding – for example, for wind and weather to be on your side. Mau and I spent it rousing the rest of our pack with our enthusiasm to star in our mini action film. We shot footage of each pilot handling gear and being cool for a series of freeze-frame introductions with their name and the country they came from written in the frame in a rugged font. Every single person was from a different country and Mau loved that, so we featured it. Then we talked everyone into wearing the same t-shirt and walking with exaggerated drama toward the camera as a group so we could edit it in slow motion for our opening sequence.

"I have an idea for my clip. I'm going to pee in the trees and you should film it," Mau said to me about the fifth day in. So I did, holding my iPhone so I could see the arc of his urine, keeping the view of his penis blocked by his back and giggling, my own bladder growing distressingly tight.

I was the only woman. A small beast in the midst of a crowd of towering men. And I had to pee.

The men peed in some scraggly bramble near the parked vans, a couple steps away from the group. But they could just turn their backs, discreetly take out their equipment, and aim. There was zero privacy available for a woman, especially one for whom peeing can accurately be described as "a scene."

I can't stand unless I use my arms to hold myself up. Which also means I can't squat. I can perch, if there is any kind of ledge at all. But then I still need something to lean against while also keeping both hands free because I have to perform, what is, technically, a sterile medical procedure to coax my bladder to release the stream. Maybe I could kind of… lie down on my side and leverage with my elbows? No. If I got out of my wheelchair and lay down alone in a field, a whole bunch of men were going to come over to see if I was okay. And I would have my pants down. I was going to need help. Since Mau and I were already essentially peeing together, I asked him to help me pee.

I found a rock to perch on, I told Mau to stand close behind me so I could lean against his shins and work out the logistics of an in-field catheterization. I finished peeing, wrapped the used catheter in the used antiseptic wipe, forced it all into the packet the wipe came in, and tucked it inside my toiletry kit.

Success! But while my bladder was much relieved, I was slightly sad. This was in no way how I imagined my underwear coming off in his presence. I also realized that I hadn't factored in the part where I would have to pull my underwear back up. How on earth would I do that without totally exposing myself? Normally, I grab the frame of my wheelchair while it's facing me and lean on it to stand, tugging up one side of my underwear and then the other, until they are over my hips and I can sit down to smooth them out. This can take an actual minute. There are no *Cosmo* articles for this situation. *How to keep it sexy when he's helping you pee!* ... try not to fully expose yourself when pulling up your underwear. If it's too late for that, be coy about it. Or: lean seductively against your wheelchair and invite him to pull your underwear up for you – be sure to maintain intense eye contact. Maybe I was supposed to fuck him first and then ask him to help me pee?

I sat on the rock, pants around my knees, leaning against Mau's shins, hoping he had not been watching me inserting thin plastic tubing inside myself. I tried to think of any other way than the only way I could think of.

"Just tell me what I can do or not to help," he said, picking up on my discomfort. He waited.

In grade four, I went to a school with a "teacher's assistant" responsible for the "special needs" of the disabled students. When there was a school trip, I had to travel with the other disabled students in the wheelchair van so Mrs. Loson could keep track of everyone. It didn't matter that I could walk, at the time, onto the big yellow bus with my classmates without specially trained supervision. I had to stay inside at recess during the winter to prevent falling or maybe from getting too cold. It didn't matter that I went home after school and played outside in the snow and ice until the streetlights came on.

It also meant that Mrs. Loson was the boss of my pee.

It is not uncommon for people who catheterize to set a schedule, generally because they don't have the sensation required to go as needed. But I can feel when I need to go so I can go when I feel like it. I had been catheterizing myself since I was in preschool, when I took the catheter from the teacher and did it myself. The preschool called my mom to make sure it was okay to let me keep going. They were cool with my independence. But at Princess Elizabeth Public School, my body wasn't up to me. Mrs. Loson arranged a schedule based on medical standards and walked to my classroom holding the plastic-wrapped disposable catheter openly in her hand. She'd gesture at me from the doorway, regardless of what classroom activity I was involved in, and walk me down the hall to the washroom with the accessible stall.

Mrs. Loson came into the stall with me, which was somehow also part of the school administration's policy. She watched me wash my hands, she watched me pull down my pants. She watched me separate my labia and swipe a sanitized towelette front to back at least twice. She watched me insert a catheter into my urethra. She listened to the stream to make sure I completely emptied my bladder. She watched me pull my pants back up and wash my hands. It didn't matter how many times I said I could, always did, and wanted to do it on my own. It was Mrs. Loson's job to watch me pee twice a day for two years. She was a warm and talented educator who invited all her kids over to her house for pool parties. I loved her. And I absolutely did not want her in the toilet stall with me.

But I had learned from a childhood full of invasive medical professionals how to go away from myself. How to pretend to be chill, laughing and joking with the strangers inserting things into me. I didn't begin to unlearn it until I was in my thirties and the things strangers were inserting in me were their penises and I was still going away from myself. I wasn't chasing intimacy, I was chasing autonomy. I believed that I had to choose.

I learned autonomy was fickle when my mother and I tried to make the supervised bathroom sessions stop. First we met with the principal.

"Please stop sending the teacher into the bathroom stall with my daughter, she's capable of handling it on her own."

"It's necessary. We're concerned she might fall off the toilet."

"Necessary to be in the stall with her?"

"Yes."

"Even though I'm asking you not to send an adult into the toilet to watch my daughter pee?"

"Oh, yes. It's not really up to you."

Ten-year-old me wrote a letter to the board of education explaining that while it was important that the board provided assistance for the students who couldn't attend to their own needs, it was a problem that help was being forced on me against my will. Help that involved regularly exposing my genitals to a teacher. Why weren't my mother and I the ones making the decision about what support I needed? The school board sent the letter to my school, who gave the letter to the nurse, who called me into her office to shame me for being ungrateful and for not understanding my place. I had to move to a new school district to attend a school without a special needs assistant so I could pee whenever I felt like it. All by myself. I learned my lesson: being helped meant giving up my personhood.

On the mountain, I took a breath. I called up the image of Mau peeing in the bushes a handful of minutes before. An image I had because he asked me to film it. Because he thought it would be a funny clip in the video we were making together. The memory – the crassness of it – put me at ease. I chose him. It was up to me. And along with the shame I expected, I was also... having fun.

"Okay. Can you lift me up by my underarms and... uh, hold me there for a second."

Mau bent down and hooked his hands under my armpits and hoisted me up like he was lifting a soaked child out of a kiddie pool. I pulled my underpants up in one quick motion.

I waited for the meanness to take over and overwhelm me with the need to get away from him in order to gather myself, but it didn't come. Letting myself be nervous and uncomfortable in front of him meant I hadn't gone away from myself in the first place. I didn't need to gather, I could just continue.

The last day of my first course of paragliding school dawned with perfect conditions for Ronda la Vieja. A place my fellow pilots had been gushing over their fond memories of all week. A place José kept mentioning, hoping the winds would be good on Friday. And it did have a glow to it. A "this is the right place" feel to it. I started crying as soon as the van doors opened. I was going to fly on my own. Adrenaline and joy kicked in the moment I saw the sweep of valley I would fly over. I thought I would be fighting anxiety at the edge, waiting for my wind. But I wasn't nervous., I had already surrendered to the sky. Mau had carried me ceremonially from my chair to my hot pink harness at the top of Ronda la Vieja, making sure someone filmed him doing it. Then he flew down ahead of me to film my whole flight. To be there when I landed. His arms were the opening and closing brackets of my first solo flight.

The takeoff came easy. One minute I was being hauled by three guys, the next I was on the wing. It was startling and I giggled. But then I settled into a deep focus. I had a flood of physical anxiety to manage, which I did by listening to José's voice on the radio. He'd been flying with me in the tandem the whole week and he knew what scared me. He assured me when he saw the dips and bumps my glider made that the movements were normal. He gave me directions. I didn't have to think or feel confident. I could be scared, I could trust, I was flying.

When I was close enough to the ground to hear his voice without the radio, I started to cry, out of pride and complete amazement. José was walking toward me as I approached; I flared on his command. I landed gently and exactly.

José grabbed the lines and tugged to bring the glider down. He straddled the styrofoam around my legs and hugged me, wiped the tears away from my face and hugged me again, all while Mau kept filming.

"That landing was impeccable!" Mau said.

"Let's see if any of these guys can land like that!" José said, pointing at the pilots still at the takeoff.

When I got home from Algodonales, I pieced together footage from my first flight that came from five different cameras, including a GoPro that captured the stoney expression on my face and how it crumpled into tears as I came into land. I couldn't help but marvel at the fact that the moment when I was the most on my own, the most free, was also the moment I was the most connected to my pack of pilot babes. Cheering at the top, waiting at the bottom, watching me all the way through.

CHAPTER FOURTEEN

Missing Pieces
Vila Seca, Spain, December 2016

FOLSOM, Brian *(March 21, 1960 - December 23, 2016).*
Loving father to Erin Clark.

Let's call that a stretch. He wasn't. Loving.

On the 23rd of December, 2016, I got a FB message from my dad's sister. 5 a.m. her time. "Hello, my dear. Can you call me?"

I glanced at the message while rolling to Expresaté, the cafe I went to every day. My Aunt and I didn't speak to each other very often, usually when someone died. I passed the stone walls of the old town, painted in a harmony of oranges and rust, echoing the hues of the Mediterranean sunsets. My wheels glided across the smooth tiles, a recent update to the city when they took out the cobblestones and narrow sidewalks in anticipation of an aging population. Roman-built buildings blended with contemporary urban design. The ease of movement to any point between my apartment and the sea felt more like belonging than anywhere else I had ever been.

The screen of my phone blinked. My mom calling. Also 5 a.m. her time. My headphones were already in, I was listening to "O Come All Ye Faithful" and rolling through the tree-lined church courtyard where the Ayuntamiento, the city hall of Vila Seca was setting up a giant Christmas tree with blue lights.

First my Aunt, then my mom. "Hi Mom. I just saw Aunt Eva's message."

"It's Brian."

I went quiet for a while.

"Are you okay?," she asked. My breath caught like I was about to cry, so I pulled on a wheel and pivoted toward a bench to take a minute. In case I needed to go back home.

"Yes." I exhaled. "I'm just surprised I care."

"It's sad. I'm sad, too."

"But why?" Tears hit my voice.

"It's Christmas. He was my first love."

The pulse of sad passed in a short minute so I just kept on to the café, chatting about nothing with my mom.

"Erin! What are these lyrics?," my friend, who was also the waitress, asked as I pulled up to the bar.

I listened to the song over the radio for a second. "Alright. I think we're gonna make it." I sang to her. She asked me to repeat it a couple times. I pulled up the lyrics on my phone to show her.

"In Spain we think the lyrics are: Alright, Pinguino Rodriguez." Everyone working behind the bar started singing and laughing and practising pronouncing "gonna."

"Say hi to them for me," my mom said, hearing the cafe ruckus. They had all met when my mom visited in October. Karina, the owner, had assured her I could always count on them for anything I needed.

"My mom says hi," I told them. The cafe said hi back in a chorus of blown kisses.

"Call me if you need me." We hung up. I didn't mention anything to my café family. I wasn't sure what it meant to me yet. "My dad died" had a heft to it I didn't want to throw around. But I felt soothed just being there, surrounded by the friendly sounds of the espresso machine, the radio playing English music, the quotidian conversations in Spanish that I was more and more able to pick up and join in with.

I was made after my mom and dad broke up. He'd sneak back to her now and then, and in that grey area of not together but still fucking, I was conceived. They each had half a rare gene that when fused together in my DNA halted the growth of my spine. I was born with pieces missing. This is both a metaphor and a reality.

When my mom told my dad she was pregnant, he got angry. Denied me. It was said he believed he was impotent. It was said that my mom had broken his heart and he was jealous and spiteful. It was said he was just an asshole. No one believed he wasn't my father, and his family carried on raising me in their midst. He carried on stubbornly indifferent to me. I carried on in a lifelong state of shock. Many awkward, unsettling moments later, he died. Not having loved me at all.

I had spent most of my life ashamed of how it had shaped me – with pieces missing.

I went looking for his obituary. *Loving father to Erin Clark.* Respecting his wish, there would be no funeral. Ignoring his assertion, I had been counted.

We drove to La Pineda. Salima, Christian, their three-year-old daughter Isabella and I. Isabella explained it was too far for me to go on my own in my "carrito," what she called my wheelchair, but we would put it in the back of the truck and all of us would go in the car together.

At the beach, we played in the sand, Isabella and I waved with delight at a remote-controlled sailboat making loops in a fountain just for us. There were sand sculptures depicting recreations of the nativity in the Catalan tradition, yet they featured interesting artistic licence: The three wise men as musicians in Hawaiian shirts and Santa beards; a lady playing piano and pooping; a family of camels. Not just camels standing around being camel-like in the usual nativity way – a mom, a dad, and a baby blissfully nuzzling, tangled in each other. It reminded me of my pilot pack. The camel jokes. Mau.

My favourite animal. Family. Shit. I was stung with sudden tenderness.

I texted a photo of the camels to Mau, who had written me a sweet and sincere Christmas wish the day before. Not wanting to feel my appreciation for him too intently, I had been flip in my response. The sand-camels broke down my defence and I texted him.

"My dad died." It felt like a confession.

"Fill your heart with empathy," he texted back, along with all his love.

Empathy? An unusual condolence, so I heard it. Like a crack.

I walked ahead of my friends back to the car. I knew a blessing that helped me get started when empathy was reluctant: May your good fortune increase. May you be happy. May you be free of all shame and suffering. May you be free of all attachment and aversion. My heart said, *okay, let's do this for your dad,* as the literal waves and my emotional waves crashed. Bold move, heart, I thought and I followed it.

The wind brushed my tears away as my friends caught up with me. Isabella ran to grab the back of my chair so she could push me. At three years old, her head barely reached the top of my backrest. I don't know how she managed to see where she was going, but I just leaned into my seat and lifted my arms from my wheels and she steered me slow and true.

I spent the next couple of days in bed, so tired I couldn't get all the way through chopping vegetables for an omelet before I got distracted, forgot what I was doing, and ended up back in bed. A childhood's worth of distant grief made its heavy way through me. I stayed still, not flinching at the bad memories.

I made a list of things that soothe me when I'm in pain. Long, quiet drives. Scrambling around in nature. Long hugs. Dancing. Sex. Singing.

Christian had loaned me his shitty acoustic guitar that lost tuning while tuning it. He had packed it in the back of the truck that same Mediterranean day, remembering me wanting one to play from months ago. I sang my heart out, off key, fuck it. I cued up "I Feel Better When I'm Dancing" on my iPhone, headphones in so as not to annoy my neighbours, and played it on repeat and danced until I was panting and my blood pulsed in tingles under my skin. I had been celibate since my divorce and had promised myself I would wait until I was emotionally connected before I had sex again, so dancing was going to count for sex.

Hugs, long drives, nature.

A few nights later, at a dinner party with friends, I couldn't hold it together anymore. I had my head down on the table by the time dessert lingered. My chest was throbbing.

"Do you want me to take you home now?" Christian asked.

"Yes. Yes, please."

"Are you only tired?," he asked in the darkness of the car. He knew my dad had died, but I had mentioned it in passing, brushing it off as neutral news. Orion was winking at me out my window.

Christian and Salima had been strangers when I first visited Vila Seca, owners of the circus studio an online acquaintance had suggested I check out while I was visiting Barcelona. I took the train, saw the gleaming tiles of the castle turret, the dry scent of the maritime pines wafting sweetly in the air, spent an unhurried afternoon tooling around on various aerial apparatus, and decided this small town would be home. Salima and Christian helped me find an apartment, open a bank account, and treated me like family. If I wasn't travelling, I was with them nearly every day. In the darkness of the truck, I held my breath. I would tell Christian how I really felt, but I had to wait for the potent impulse to just say "Yeah, I'm fine" to pass.

"No," I sobbed. The truck hummed. I sucked snot back into my nose. Christian handed me a wad of paper towel. I kept on sobbing.

We pulled up in front of my apartment half an hour later.

"Do you want to say anything about it?" he asked.

I shook my head and hiccuped. I didn't know how to start. "Are you getting a cold?" I asked him instead when he coughed. He told me how he had been tired lately, about the things that had been causing him stress, the feelings he had been chewing on since the last time we had a heart-to-heart. I shifted my body to listen to him.

"Your turn," he said when he was done talking.

"I got nothing," I said, still struggling against myself to open up.

He pressed on. "I'm confused. The picture I saw on FB of someone who died ten years ago, I thought that was your dad."

"That was my stepdad."

"He was good with Barbies?" he asked, referencing the picture I had posted with my stepdad holding a gaggle of Barbies in his arms.

"He was good with me," I smiled. Tony had let me take that picture because I had laughed so hard at him herding Barbies I was too old to enjoy myself. I started talking. Christian listened and let the night drain. Salima was waiting for him back at the party, an hour of driving away, but he knew she would understand, so he listened and I told him about my other dad. The one who never wanted me.

When I got inside, I got a text from my mom: "Erin, I don't know if you are going to write about this, but if you do, I'm okay with whatever information you choose to share. This will be part of my healing as well. No more shame for something that happened decades ago and brought my children into my life."

No more shame.

Love had been as scarce as moisture in the desert and I had tried to be like the Namib Desert beetle when it came to love. They draw water from fog, from deep mist, no actual rain, just vapour of water, the *idea* of moisture out of arid and thin air. The texture of their skin attracts water, then bumps on their back form a pattern that run the droplets, *The Price Is Right* Plinko style, right to their mouth. They sip at water that doesn't exist for other creatures, sustaining themselves and, in turn, sustaining life around them.

In the same desert, settlers had planted groves of non-indigenous trees in the wild plots of land they occupied. The trees provided a practical windbreak around settlements and a sense of nostalgia for far-from-home foreigners, but they also suck up precious ground water.

I heard of one man in particular who had an oak tree in his yard in the middle of the Namib Desert. He loved how unlikely it was to even be there in the first place, and he happily paid extra on his water bill to keep it luscious and green. The local environmentalists, however, would happily have seen all the town's trees uprooted.

The truth was, I didn't *want* to be a beetle. I wanted to be an oak tree. A tree doesn't resent having needs. Needs make you vulnerable, reliant on people who may never meet them. It is smarter to be a beetle than an oak tree. And while no one wanted to see me uprooted more than myself, I was, unbeknownst to myself, searching for a friendly yard where the delightful unlikeliness of me was worth whatever I might cost to maintain.

In Vila Seca, I was loved like that, by Salima and Christian and the family at the café, by the unlikely wheelchair accessibility of the town itself. Love wasn't scarce, it wasn't an immense or desperate effort. It was unlikely for me to be there –123 kilometres from Barcelona, in a town with no attractions, one of the very few foreigners around – and maybe exactly for that reason, they watered me.

CHAPTER FIFTEEN

A Good Match
Vila Seca, Spain, July 2016

Mau was in Spain to paraglide in the Pyrenees with José, and on his way through he came to visit me in Vila Seca. I met him at my local station. We had gotten closer over WhatsApp – I had confessed that I had feelings for him, and he had made this plan to go out of his way to see me. I wasn't warmed up yet when he arrived, but he was full of enthusiasm as we walked to my apartment. I had written an essay about him helping me pee. Not only had it been published in a literary journal, it had won an award for non-fiction. He was so proud of me. He loved the essay about us peeing in the mountains. After we got to my place, he gave me a beautiful necklace – the green, iridescent wings of a Costa Rican butterfly, ethically harvested after a natural death, and pressed between lucite. He teased me about turning down his kiss on the last day.

"You tried to kiss me?" I was surprised. I remembered folding myself into him for a goodbye cuddle.

"You turned me down," he said. Then I remembered all those kisses on my cheek – for I had given him my cheek when he leaned toward me. "I took it as you telling me it wasn't going to happen like that for us."

"No, not like that," I agreed. If I was going to kiss him, it would be to start something, not end it.

"I was being cautious, too," he said. "With sex, it's like, you're into that first time with different kinds of people. I was aware of not wanting to fetishize you like that."

I had suspected many lovers of doing that. I had suspected several men who were strange and distant physically but intimate emotionally of struggling with that. I had very few times brought it up. Not once had a potential sexual partner brought it up with me.

We talked for hours, mostly about his love life and how he had recently sabotaged it. I took him to Expresaté, showed him my favorite corners of Vila Seca, and then we headed back to my apartment.

"I need to lie down," I said. I had strict limits of how much time my back could tolerate sitting up.

We pulled a fresh sheet over my bed together, tucking in our respective corners. He lay down on his back and opened his arms for me to lie against him. I breathed him in, the same sweet and woodsy scent as when we met, and settled.

"I feel like I can't come out fully as bisexual until I'm in a relationship, a happy ending," he said. He had been so immediate and insistent with his bisexuality with me when we first met that I hadn't realized it wasn't common or public knowledge. He radiated distress at how impossible a happy ending seemed for him.

"I don't think there's such a thing as one, big, happy ending. I think there are just all kinds of little ones. Millions happening all the time," I said. It was a general philosophy of mine, to not be focused so much on endings as more immediate moments, and the easy pleasures in them. I can get so obsessive, so destructively self-loathing, I can't spend too long in a hunt for salvation in the form of achievements. *I'll feel safe when I own a home. I'll finally like myself when I am a professional.* I had learned that even when those moments came, the relief I had waited for wasn't with them. I was still unsettled. To keep it from spiralling, I focused on what made me feel safe and happy as it occurred, not on what would make it a permanent state. I felt safe and happy in Mau's arms.

"You say there are millions, but I don't see any," he said, his voice cracking, my head rising and sinking where it rested against him as he sighed in defeat.

"This is one right now." My arm was draped across his chest. I said my words into his shoulder. It was so rare to feel affection like this, so physical. The link of his hand gently grasping my wrist soothed me instead of agitated me. I wanted to feel all the ways Mau would grasp me, all the ways we could make a link between us. "Think of the happenstance of us meeting in the first place," I continued. "Think of the immense geographical distance between us. Think of all the things we've been through in the last eight months that could have easily distanced us further, but here we are. And I love you so much."

"Same," he barely said, exhaling heavily, glancing at me briefly from the side of his eyes and rolling his gaze away from the risk of it.

"Whatever this is, it isn't fragile," I said, feeling certain of myself.

And we napped, fully clothed, his body a still and solid frame around me.

When we woke up, I told him an idea I'd had for ages.

"People tell me all the time what a pity it is that I'm beautiful since no one will want me because I'm disabled. Mostly, I think, because they just don't see evidence of it. We get so much of our ideas about romance from movies, but the only time I saw a wheelchair in a romantic movie, it was the one where the guy kills himself in the end so he won't be a burden to his girlfriend. And his death was rendered as a noble, romantic gesture. I am sure I can do better than that. I want to recreate iconic romantic movie scenes with my wheelchair in them."

"I love that idea! I'd love to do that with you," Mau said. "Hey, do you want to take selfies now?"

An hour before his train, we set up in the courtyard of my apartment building. We had no idea how to pose, no idea of what we were going for. I synced my remote shutter, set the camera up, and called him to me. We were talking to each other and I was leaning on him as I pressed the shutter button. I expected the photos to be a lot of awkward shots of us looking tense and unsure of each other; instead, the whole series came out as posed and sweet as engagement photos.

We switched places and Mau sat in my wheelchair, I climbed onto his lap. I felt something click into place when I settled my body against Mau while he was sitting in my wheelchair. Me against him. Him around me. And something inside. I could see the "click" that I felt in the photos – it was like picking a matching pair in a game of memory. There was all of the pride at remembering where the pair was; there was that fulfilling reassurance to see the match itself.

How much does being in a body I can't entirely feel contribute to my sense of unreality – this feeling that I am so often searching for matches between me and the world? I can name the series of experiences I think taught me how to disconnect, but what of the impact of the numbness with which I was born? I cannot feel most of my body from my waist down. In terms of paralysis, I am medically referred to as "incomplete." If I place my feet on the ground, they send no feedback to my brain about the ground. My wheels usually mediate between me and my environment. But my wheels don't feel the ground either. What I can feel is often muted and indirect. The sensation that is intact is hyper-intense. Even surreal.

It's not just an issue of my identity being challenged and erased by how society treats me or how I was raised. It's also that half of my body isn't a felt reality to me because I can't feel it.

It is like I live in a dream of being disembodied, of floating above my body and looking back at it. My legs are dream legs doing dream things. I am looking down at them, but I am not in them. What I imagine has the same sense of reality as what I can see. I construct ideas about what my legs are doing and how it might feel by what I can see them doing, from the patches of sensation I do have.

It's common for people to construct ideas about what they can do and how it might feel by watching other people who look more or less like them do things. What if no one doing anything looks like you at all? Then you must be your own evidence. Construct a life from what you can imagine, from your other senses reaching out into the world and bringing its details back to you. Make it vivid and thorough, but not delusional. Fantasy is not reality.

But it can become real. They can match.

Later that summer, Mau suggested I write a post to go with some of the more romantic selfies we took. And I did. I wrote about how nice it was to feel shy with someone. To feel so tender and full of hope that it made me feel shy. Which meant I didn't feel defensive. I was open to something. On Instagram people texted flame emojis and hearts and gushed about how sweet we were together. After posting it to Facebook where all his friends and family could also read it and see it, Mau texted me: "You know what I just realized? The fact that you posted my comment about 'future husband or wife' is the first time that my bisexuality is "publicly" printed somewhere."

"...Uh yeah. Want me to take it out?" I texted back.

"Nope. I actually LⓄⓄⓄVE it," he replied.

"I love it, too. It was exactly the way you first told me you were bi. Wouldn't be right without it. How does it feel?" I asked.

"It feels pretty "whatever," which is FUCKING AWE-SOME," he replied.

I took screengrabs of the comments people were leaving on Instagram and sent them to him.

"Am I misunderstanding something or do people think we're together?," he asked.

"Yes, they think we're together. Are you surprised by that? I'll take it down if you want. I feel bad," I typed.

"Why do you feel bad?," he asked.

"No good reason," I texted. I couldn't explain it to myself – why would I feel bad? But there it was, a constricting in my throat, a little squeeze in my gut, a nervous flush on my skin.

CHAPTER SIXTEEN

Please, No Difficult Wind
Algodonales, Spain, March 2017

Five months after my first flying course, I went back for another week. José had bought a buggy. A low-riding, three-wheeled metal frame fitted with the same harness everyone else flies in. My legs were protected by the frame, and my torso was free.

The takeoff at Lucena is so steep it took José, Pablo, and another pilot, Matteo, to get me off the ground. When I saw the incline, the idea of my wheels being nose-down while we waited for a solid wind made my throat lurch.

"Erin, I leave it up to you," José said. My options were to fly it or drive back down to the landing site and hope for enough wind to practise ground handling.

My mind calculated the wind, tracked the patch of landing at the crossroads, took in the vastness. My heart begged me to rethink my life with its pounding. Or maybe it was begging me to fling myself into it. Sometimes it can be hard to tell. One leap into the unknown – a divorce, for example – leads to other precipices. You have to keep choosing to fly or drive back down to the safety of the landing field.

I chose to fly.

I slid down the slope on my butt to the edge. Matteo stood in front of the buggy, holding it in place by resting the frame on his thigh. It was so steep Pablo had to press my shoulder back against the harness so I could buckle it up across my chest. And then the wind died.

Low wind involves running until the wing is aloft. Without running, I have less time to make corrections, and those corrections need to be flawless.

"Please, no difficult wind," I pleaded.

"If you don't have control, we don't let you go," José said.

As a team, we tried again and again to keep the wing up and over my head. As the adrenaline mixed with frustration, tears started to run down my cheeks.

Seeing them, José said, "If you are that scared, we should stop."

"No. If I just let the tears out, I can keep my body relaxed," I assured him. "I'm okay."

"I don't have it. I don't have it," I said each time, getting none of the tension in the line that tells you the wing is inflated. That it's flying. We'd all bring the wing down. My heart started to give up. I undid all the buckles of the harness and crawled back up the slope to let other pilots take off.

"I couldn't get control," I told José, feeling like the weak link in the takeoff team.

"It's good for me to hear you say that. Because I know you are feeling your glider and you won't do something dangerous," José reassured me. And then we set up at the edge again.

This time, a gust came for me. I screamed as I shot straight up. José and the guys reached above their heads to keep hold of me.

"Take control!" José shouted. I tugged the lines until I felt tension, pulling on the left side, then the right, to keep the wing centred above my head.

"I have it. It's me! I have it!" I called triumphantly, and they let go.

"You can cry as much as you want now!" José teased me over the radio, and I burst into an exultant sob before collecting my wits. This flight would also be my first unassisted landing.

"Okay, Erin. It's Javi at the landing. You're going to land without instruction. You'll hear from me only if you need correction." The radio went silent.

The part of flying where you are just high and have no major decisions to make can be surprisingly dull. With exposure, the novelty and fear wears off, your reactions to shifts in the wing become more automatic, and you are simply, no big deal, flying. It was this exact feeling I wanted, the reason I did this terrifying and stressful thing. When I was so relaxed I could get bored, then I would have the natural urge to go higher or faster or farther away from the mountain. It occurred to me that despite my tendency to take big risks and lean into fear, I was chasing a serene command of the situation, not the adrenaline I had to work through to get there. If I could feel peaceful hundreds of metres above the ground, certainly I could feel peaceful for other, more commonly terrifying things. Falling in love, pursuing big creative dreams and ambitions, life in general.

When I had lost enough height, I headed for the landing, making my choices. I could see where Javi was standing, the wind would lead to him, I aimed in that direction and made giant S turns to stay in place over the landing field as I lost height, then settled in for a final stretch, a straight line until I hit ground.

"I want to hug you!" Javi joked when I was close enough to hear him from the ground, his arms wide as if to catch me right out of the air.

I had been the first to land all week, so there had been no one to video me. "I really want to see it, Javi," I rued each time, after taking my praise for my smooth and controlled landings. This time, as I came in for the final, Javi called to the other students at all corners of the landing area, "Everybody! Get your phones out!" All the pilots in the field pulled their phones out and took video of me from every angle.

Javi did actual somersaults on his way over to me after I came to a flawless stop in the flat, grassy field.

Later that night, José told me how brave he thought I was. He actually stopped the van to make sure I understood he didn't mean because of my wheelchair. He thought I was brave because of the learning curve of the buggy.

"I think we are learning very fast. And by 'we,' I mean all of us together. Everyday, we learn something new, but you're the one who has to actually fly. Today was our most difficult place we take off."

"I *felt* brave," I said.

I complained a lot about the restrictions I felt. The buggy had solved the need to be carried and was more comfortable than the feeling of being zippered into a coffin, the "race car" I had learned in. But now that I was comfortable, I wanted more of the action for myself. Whenever I would take off, three instructors were involved. One to push and two to lift and control my glider. This also meant that I rarely did ground handling.

I was three weeks into pilot training and had never lifted my own glider, so I was never sure what I was doing right or wrong.

"I need to lift my own glider," I would insist. But someone would always discourage me, saying, "It's too heavy, we're helping to control it, we do this for other pilots, too." But then I would watch a field full of brand-new pilots, one or two days into their training, running back and forth in the fields with their inflated gliders, left to work it out for themselves.

"I know you want to do this on your own," Javi said to me on the first ground-handling day. His eyes glittered with my favourite empathy, the kind that understands the glory of figuring something out for one's self.

"The idea that I'm not strong enough to lift the glider is dumb," I said to him.

"I agree. I know you're strong. You just need someone to give you a push, and I have an idea."

We set up at the edge of the practice field, where there was a slight downward slope, a couple metres away from the young sunflower crop that would act as a natural bumper if I got any speed. Javi spread my wing out behind me and showed me again how to clip into my harness. Usually this is a task students learn and are responsible for on their first day, but it so often was done for me that I kept forgetting how to do it correctly by myself.

The wind was light and calm, and I was eager. The buggy was so low to the ground that the only way Javi could really get a grip was by crouching down and grabbing the front wheel. When a breeze came, he took a backward lunge and tugged me with his body weight while I pulled on the lines. They went taut in my hands, the canvas of the risers pressed into my bare skin over my biceps, which were flexed hard against the tension of the wing. The weight of the wing went through my whole body. Where pilots would lean their chests forward and begin to run, all I had were my arms, shoulders tugged back, the muscles of my chest squeezing, and Javi pulling. And then the wing was up. Briefly, and lopsided. And then it collapsed around us. Javi fell back on his butt, laughing.

"That's it, my girl! We did it!," he shouted and unclipped me to reset the glider so we could try again.

Again and again, Javi pulled me and I lifted the glider, feeling how my body set itself against the force of it, slowly learning the subtleties of lifting it and controlling it. After an hour, we could get it overhead, Javi jogging slowly toward the sunflower field while I flew it like a kite. Javi tumbled over and again into the plants to stop my buggy. We were giddy.

José wandered over and we set up again to show him what we had accomplished. José set himself beside me, prepared to lift the glider for me.

"No, José, she does it all herself," Javi said.

"You've been helping her," José pointed out.

"I haven't touched the wing this entire time, I just pull the buggy," Javi retorted.

"José, go stand over there and watch!" I bossed him proudly. He trudged off to the far side and shrugged, pretending to not believe it could be done.

"Ready?" Javi called.

"Ready!" I squealed.

The glider swooshed to life against my arms, now marked from the rub and scrape of the harness and the canvas of the risers. Javi jogged a little faster, and as I held the wing above my head, the buggy lifted slightly off the ground. I was flying, maybe two inches off the ground.

"Perfect takeoff!" José exclaimed. "Woah! Now I see you don't need me!" he teased.

It was the best thing he could have said to me. After that, at the takeoff, José would remind the guys that I only needed a push. I pulled the glider up on my own.

I had been flying for three weeks, but I was just beginning. I was downright arrogant about my badass landings in my buggy, but the takeoffs intimidated me. Not just for being the most dangerous part of paragliding, but I was doing a lot of things differently. Holding the risers differently, my body position was different, I had to be as in sync with the person pushing me as anyone else had to be with the wind. When it worked, I felt lucky, and when it didn't, I tortured myself, trying to figure out what had gone wrong. Now I was more independent, which is what I had wanted. And, irritatingly, now that I had what I wanted, of course part of me missed the comfort of all those hands on my lines, doing it for me.

A couple days later, we were flying from Levante, a more familiar takeoff. I was halfway across the ridge when Pablo came on the radio. "Erin, turn to the right, 360 degrees to the right."

It was an unusual instruction. Normally, they tell me to keep my hands up so I fly faster, to make sure I clear the mountain, the road, and the power lines between the takeoff and the landing site.

"Erin, keep turning." I followed his instruction obediently: it may have been weird, but it was clear. Pablo knew I wanted to work on my turns, so maybe the idea was to practise them here, where the air is bumpy and I would have much to learn.

But halfway through the first turn, I realized what he'd done. I was in lift.

A thermal is a column of rising air. When your wing hits it, it lifts you up. As a beginner, you keep a tight control of your glider to manage the turbulence as you cross the threshold of a thermal and move through it. But if you turn at the right moment, and with the right radius, you spiral up it. Higher. Higher.

"Keep turning," Pablo said while I squealed and giggled and screamed. "Keep turning."

Oh god, oh god. I could feel the rise in my stomach. And the tiny hairs on my arms.

"Keep turning. Ok, you got it!" Pablo exulted.

I was above the takeoff and rising.

"You can stay with it on your own now," Pablo said. I overheard José in the background tell him I might be scared in the thermal, to stay with me so I wouldn't give up. And I was scared. Terrified in a way that is also excitement.

And, oh god, I was still rising.

Feelings overwhelmed me before height did, and I took myself out of the thermal and headed for the landing field.

The euphoria imprinted the flight in me. My body soared. I listened to my blood rush through my ears like the wind all the rest of the day. Still rushing hours later as I fell asleep.

Now that I was handling my own wing, the increase in independence made me aware of the limits of the buggy. It had tiny wheels, spread far apart, impossible to push myself in, which meant I was trapped at the landing.

Pepe's landing bar is a fold-out table set up behind Pepe's silver hatchback, where he serves cold beers and sodas out of coolers. The local pilots keep in close contact as they scan the weather forecasts for the most flyable site, and Pepe would arrive at dusk, wherever we had convened, so we could finish our day of flying with something cold and refreshing. I'd sit in the shade, having been pulled or carried there, drinking an ice-cold lemon Aquarius and stuck in place until my wheelchair – my independence – arrived with the van. I'd puzzle over this strange mix of the total freedom of flight bracketed by the severe restriction to my mobility on the ground.

I'm terrified of heights. My heart pounds, my body shivers from adrenaline, it takes an immense amount of energy to focus my mind into calmness during takeoff and flight. Fear is also what makes it exhilarating. I yearn to command myself beyond an otherwise reasonable limit. I don't face my fear of heights to paraglide because I'm content being confined.

One day during that week, a car pulled up next to me at the landing site, and a pilot's wife I recognized from the takeoff hopped out. "My husband just called me from the takeoff and said that your chair is there, but the van is not." We called whoever was driving the van to ask if they had my chair. They did not. They had to drive back up to get it.

To fly, I transfer from my wheelchair to the buggy; someone else then has to remember to put the wheelchair back in the van before driving down to collect us from the landing field. It was easy to forget; no one else was dependent on it. But without it, I was helpless.

The skills I needed to conquer my fear of heights were between me and my instructors. What I needed to get around on my own before and after flight was between me and my equipment. While it's a common misconception in the minds of able-bodied people that someone in a wheelchair dreams of being able to walk, my dreams were filled with sensations of flight and the physics of the wing and my body, except my body is also my wheelchair. If I was going to have independence in this sport, I was going to need to fly the body I used to get around on the ground. Just like everybody else.

I still had my old wheelchair, the one that snapped the day sepsis took over my body, the one that heralded my divorce, that three-wheeled death trap wheelchair. I asked Luisma: If I brought that to Spain, would he retrofit it into something I could fly? I hadn't seen many of the adaptations other disabled pilots used, but I knew what we had been trying and what we were learning from it. My instructors were skeptical about the practicality of flying a wheelchair, based on the way they struggled when they would play in my chair on the ground, trying to do wheelies and falling backward and sideways. But what they didn't realize is that they struggled because they had no wheelchair skills. I was sure I would be able to move my wheelchair with the same ease and agility as other pilots had when they hopped and twisted around under their wings.

A flying wheelchair seemed like a reasonable request to me. Luisma agreed.

Luisma examined the rusted and shattered skeleton of my old chair. I expected him to sand down the jagged metal edge where the wheel had snapped and attach the new all-terrain wheel I'd bought. I figured the real work would be attaching a harness to the frame. But Luisma saw it differently. He saw rusted bolts and wouldn't send me up in the air in a dirty old divorce beast. He spread a piece of cardboard on the floor of the paragliding school and got to work. He dismantled the entire thing until it was a pile of unrecognizable parts. I watched him ease apart joints I didn't even know were separate pieces. I felt the release in my own bones. He did saw and smooth off the jagged gash where the wheel had snapped off the frame. He measured, cut, and welded the new, more rugged wheel securely in place. He nursed my old chair back to life with an unbroken focus for hours at a time. After I finished my paragliding holiday, he continued to work on it for months. All the while, I was back at home, dreaming about the movements, the feel, the poetry, of a wheelchair in flight.

PART THREE

ALL FALL DOWN

The entry is always easier than we think, not knowing what we're getting ourselves into. It's the exit that re-quires a risk. Little Tell me everything. *Little* Not in a million years [...] *How much pleasanter to recount the* rosie *and not the* all fall down.

—*RISK: AN ACCOUNTING,*
BRENDA MILLER AND JULIE MARIE WADE

CHAPTER SEVENTEEN

Love All the Way
Bogotá, Colombia, November 2017

When I was a kid, I was part of a United Pentecostal congregation. My grandparents and my beloved babysitter, Liz, would get the Holy Spirit on Wednesday nights and Sunday mornings. It would possess them so completely their bodies would shake, they would dance around the pews and speak in tongues. I would not. I wanted to be consumed so desperately, I would think about how I could imitate their actions, but then I would know I was faking it, and that couldn't be the Holy Spirit. God's love should overtake you. But no matter how much I prayed that the Holy Spirit would come into me, I never felt it. I was unworthy. Never ecstatic.

Days before my dad died, my witchy friend Camelia received the tattooed skull of a goat as a gift and posted to Facebook that her and her magic goat skull were available to perform rituals for release from bad love.

My desire for love felt like praying for the Holy Spirit. I was calling for an immense force of romantic determination to rip me open and make me take it. What I carried was a primal fear. God had abandoned me. Both of my fathers had abandoned me. In my marriage I had abandoned me. What would it take to feel a sense of security deep enough that when the opportunity came, I could really let go? When I really considered it, what seemed to be missing was commitment. I didn't feel loved, my logic went, because none of the love I had went all the way.

"Hey, Camelia? Um, I know that the skull is supposed to help with love that has gone wrong. But what about love that doesn't go all the way? Can it help with that?," I messaged her.

"I love this," she wrote. "I will ask."

When Camelia said she would ask, she meant a deck of tarot cards would speak – in imagery – on behalf of the skull. When she asked the goat skull if it could help me find love that goes all the way, it said: the Chariot, the Pope, the Empress.

"You can teach Erin to exchange her wheelchair for a throne," Camelia interpreted. "Okay. The Empress is a consort, not a single woman, so I'll go forward with it. To be on the safe side," she then said, and asked the skull via the cards, "is there anything specific about this ritual?" The skull gave her the Emperor.

In the Marseille tarot deck, the Empress sits holding a shield that looks like a wheel to one side. Her expression is fierce, her posture commands, drawing all she requires and desires to her. The Emperor stands. His arm at rest on his belt. His leg kicked back with a very imperial ease, his heel resting on a shield that also looks like a wheel. When the cards are back to back, the Empress has wheels on each side. When the Emperor stands with her, her throne is a wheelchair. A true power couple. A good omen for my love-all-the-way ritual.

In November of 2017, when the alimony period ran out, I went to New York to close the joint bank account Elliott and I shared. I asked Mau if we could meet in New York while I was there as he was often in the city for work. Instead, he invited me to visit him in Bogotá. At the last minute, he asked if I wanted to do the romantic movie photo shoot with him. The one I had told him about when he visited me. I was nervous. This felt serious – I was invited to a foreign country to stay with a man I had feelings for, and we would recreate romantic movie scenes, with me as the romantic and desirable heroine and with my wheelchair visible because I had told him how much that kind of imagery would have meant to my self-esteem growing up. During the day, Mau worked and I toured Bogotá. In the evenings we dressed up as classic movie stars and pretended to be passionately in love. Only, it wasn't entirely pretend. After the photographer cleared out his gear and left us, Mau would take off my costume and we'd make love, falling asleep with our bodies entwined, Mau's hands grasping my legs, stroking my shoulders, smoothing my hair, interlacing his fingers with my fingers, and holding me the length of an entire night, every night. I was basking in an incredible sense of connection.

The morning of my last day in Colombia, I was feeling like we had something good, something worth pursuing. I had let go in a way I had never been able to before, and it felt euphoric. We were eating breakfast in the hotel dining room that we had turned into the set of one of our photo shoots a few nights before. I assumed Mau was feeling the same glow, but at some point he said, " I feel like I can't let myself love all the way." And my first thought was: LOVE ALL THE WAY! Oh, the glorious mystical fate of that exact wording!

Wait, *can't*?

Oh. Fuck.

My expression fell so dramatically as he talked that he paused and said, "I didn't bring this up as a way to talk about us. But should we have the talk?"

I did not want to have the talk, not *this* talk. This was the talk I had been warned about my entire life. *No one will want you.* But he *had* wanted me. He'd been wanting me the whole year leading up to this, right? I did not want to hear how it wasn't enough. I wanted him to reach for me across the table, flick his finger against my wrist as he spoke the way he sometimes did. Couldn't he just say, on that morning of all mornings, fresh off making love, *something* affectionate? I would have been happy with a simple, "How are you?," acknowledging that he knew something important had happened to me. I realize now that these were all things I could have, *should* have said, on my own behalf at the time, but I didn't. I said, "Yes, maybe we should have the talk." We left the dining room in a somber march and headed back to his room.

"You start the conversation," he said. We took up opposite sides of his king-sized bed. He sat cross-legged, and I lay on my back.

Where were we?

What he had actually said that morning was: "I feel like I can't let myself love all the way. I like the love stories where they don't end up together, like *Casablanca*." That was one of the movies we had recreated. "Where they love each other but they can't be together. I feel pretty cynical about love, actually."

I had spent my entire graduating year of high school obsessively fantasizing about lovers who loved each other but couldn't be together. If I wanted to strongarm an oversimplified connection, I could say that being cynical about love was the reason I didn't graduate. It was the reason I married Elliott. But even without those links, I hated cynicism. It made my fear feel smart, but it made my heart feel dead.

"People who love each other but can't be together" was a love story to which I had been relegated. It was the best-case scenario: He loves me, that's true and real. But since I'm still disabled, we can't expect that to work out happily ever after. I knew that in this situation with Mau, and in my life in general, my wheelchair had very little to do with it, but I'd seen that specific narrative play out in movies and TV shows in which disability or illness was at the crux of it, but it also affected me if the reason was war, or religion, or distance, or stupidity. My chest would heave at the moment the lovers had to part like it was happening to me. It wasn't a narrative I *liked*, but it was a narrative that felt personal.

I was scornfully unimpressed by those movies on principal. What made them so much more realistic than love that actually worked out for someone like me?

The photo shoot had been my private, somewhat hesitant, act of defiance. Now it had grown bolder. And we had done it together. It wasn't just the stigma of dating and disability we were defying but also every single insecure thought that stops any of us from letting ourselves love and be loved. I wasn't about to just shrug and say, "Well, that was nice, back to the usual, I guess."

I took a deep breath. "It's so weird to me that you feel cynical about falling in love because I'd swear that we are."

"We have really been Mr. and Mrs. this week," he agreed. "This doesn't mean more to you than it does to me, but I don't want to be in a long-distance relationship."

This. Did he mean the sex? The photoshoot? Or the whole passionate, heady, magnetic flirtation – the emotional consummation? I had the impression that the sex was not that big of a deal to Mau. Not just sex with me, but also in general. He was breathtakingly casual about it, texting me about "accidental threesomes" in the course of updating me about his weekend. Instead of jealousy, it made me feel safer about being emotionally intimate with him. I knew that was weird, but it worked. But if we were on the same page about how meaningful this was emotionally, why did it remind me of what Elliot had told me: "Sometimes it can just wear off after you… get what you want."

Looking back, I think this is the moment I would have cried or stormed out in astonishment and anger if I hadn't been so numb. The moments when I'm mostly likely to dissociate are not when I'm scared, or when something is dangerous, or even when I'm sad. What cuts me off from myself the most is the fear of humiliation. And being naive about men and romance is humiliating. I was trying to have a conversation about a relationship, but I wasn't sure I understood what a relationship was, how it functioned, when it even existed. Instead of expressing how I felt (I had no idea in that moment anyway), I tried to gather intel.

Like a reporter, I asked, "What about the photos? When I share the photos, when I write about this?" I knew I was going to write about what had happened between us. The point of the photos was to share them. How was that supposed to work if he was dating other people? At this point, the energy in the room shifted from a heavy emotional humidity to a crackling, drier air. As if on cue, Mau started to put his suit on to go to work, answering my questions as he buttoned up his shirt and chose a tie, sitting back down on the bed to pull on his socks.

"What if you meet someone else? What if you meet someone who wants to do photoshoots and write about your relationship?" I asked, as if the work needed more protection than my heart.

"Erin, I doubt I'll meet anyone else like you," Mau replied.

"People thought we were together before when I posted about us..." I persisted in inquiry.

"Everything you wrote was true, though," he said.

Mau and I needed a script. Like Laura and I had written for ourselves to say goodbye. We needed to be able to stop time and figure this out carefully. Instead we were careening full speed ahead, the conversation was incomprehensible. Were we breaking up? Was he acknowledging that we had been together? I tried to discern a pattern, to link what we were saying to how everything felt, but it was just live wires and nonsense.

Yet instead of interpreting the confusion as an answer in its own right, I was driven by an obsessive need to understand what exactly didn't add up. If I could figure it out, I could reconcile it and feel at ease again. Connected again. It didn't occur to me that another option, when something feels off, is to leave it alone, to understand that it isn't for you, and that this can bring its own kind of ease. I have spent my whole life forging my way around other people's limits; I don't let go easily. Why would it be any different, being determined for Mau's heart, as it was being determined to fly?

Sensing that I was trying to get at something and failing, Mau asked genuinely, "What would ideally happen between us after you leave?"

Camelia's tarot reading was in the back of my mind, but I didn't say, "Uh, love all the way, actually. Those exact words. I had a witch get her magic goat skull to help me find it once." Instead I said, "I want this to continue to grow," believing there was room for that.

I wanted to keep creating together. The way he was loving me through my art was fulfilling a need I hadn't even known I had. I was thinking of all the selfies I had been sending him, the pieces of writing he read and commented on. The stories I texted about my daily life that were only for him to read. The photos and stories he texted me back. That was an intimacy that filled me. If he was agreeing to that, I figured, maybe I would be satisfied.

One morning in Bogotá Mau was choosing a dress shirt, buttoning it up, fixing the sleeves. I loved being there as he dressed and undressed, the markers of the beginning and end of a regular day.

"Do you believe in God?" he asked, without context, almost as casually as if he were asking if I could pass him his tie. I paused.

Intimacy charged the room, the bed-couch-table, all-in-one-room configuration like the set of a play. Everything happens here. The sexual tension thrummed with an aura of intensity and expectation, expectation that made me feel at the limit of any previously known vulnerability. All this was mixed with the quiet intimacy of him getting ready for work while dropping big-deal questions like it was no big deal – it all made my heart flip. This is what any day would feel like between us if we chose this relationship. I lost all sense of my answer to the reverie.

I stopped going to church when I was in my twenties. I got into paganism; I meditated and learned reiki; I got tarot readings, and spiritual healings, and lit candles. My soul needed ways to pray, to access a sense of spirit in my life without the church's requirements, so I tossed off the idea that god could have any requirements of us. God was another dad who had let me down. I was really and truly a woman of my own. Which was not a triumph, it was lonely. Until I felt, a sliver at a time, that the bliss of surrender to the mystery, the joyful oneness I thought my family and friends were experiencing as they shouted praise and stomped their feet, was a feeling to which I had access. Perhaps my version was quieter, more internal, more nature-induced, but it was not withheld. Maybe love was just as available, but I'd been looking for the wrong signs.

The photos we took recreating the poster for *Mr. and Mrs. Smith* arrived a month or so after I left Bogotá. We'd posed separately and left it to the photographer to put us together. Instead of photoshopping the name "Smith" down the centre so we both appear to be leaning against it, he put us back-to-wheelchair-back.

In the photo Mau is standing with his leg kicked back, heel resting on my wheel, hand in his pocket with the mix of ease and command an Emperor might possess.

I am sitting, my expression fierce with the air of someone who expects the things she desires and requires to come to her. The expectation of an Empress.

My wheelchair was a throne. It was a sign. The pattern of our relationship restored. It fuelled me with optimism.

CHAPTER EIGHTEEN

Mad or Wise?
Mussoorie, India, April 2018

Sarah and I met at the Iceland Writers Retreat in April 2017. She was standing behind me in the line for the shower room at the Blue Lagoon when they came to take me, alone, to a more accessible changeroom and I hesitated. The waterproof wheelchair the lagoon provided was like a giant stroller, I could not get from the showers to the lagoon if I was alone.

Despite this being our first interaction, Sarah could sense my discomfort. "Do you want me to come with you?" she asked. I nodded, feeling rescued, and she ducked out of line and we followed the lagoon employee. We were left in a room that was both shower station and first-aid station. We got naked together ten minutes after making acquaintance.

There was a full moon the next night, and we joined the bus trip trying to catch the Northern Lights. They did not show, but as we waited, I ended up telling Sarah how I had just met a man who I adored and I couldn't shake the feeling that there was – would be – a story to tell. At that point in time, nothing more than being carried out of a field of sunflowers and being hand-fed grapes had even happened, Mau and I had only spent that one week of paragliding together, but I could feel it coming. I could feel a book writing itself in me as I got to know Mau and it freaked me out. It was something I could only say to another writer. It was a conference full of people with books inside them – people who narrated the events of their lives as they unfolded; who were scared; who had no idea where translating their ideas and visions into words would lead them, what it would cost, how it would change them if they dared to write.

We stood in the freezing Icelandic air under a full moon so bright we could see volcanic ridges in the distance.

"I think that's going to be an amazing book," she said. And I began to believe her.

By the next year, Sarah had moved to India with her husband and kids. I had started writing down every detail of what had happened between Mau and me in Bogotá. It wasn't a book, maybe a very long essay. I wanted to write it like a movie and to include the photos we had taken in the text. I was buzzing with story, it was all I could think about. Mau had fuelled me, this story was changing me. But along with the passion of creation, there was an equally electric anxiety.

That November, after I returned home to Spain, panic attacks kept me up at night. I was worried about money, processing the fundamental shift in my financial security after the end of a generous amount of alimony. But it wasn't just money. I was on the verge of the biggest creative undertaking I had ever approached. Passion and panic took turns in my brain. I tried to manage the anxiety by focusing on the shifts of the story I was telling about the love into which I had fallen. What would happen after this section, and then the next section, and when the piece was finished? Those were questions I could answer. Where I was asking the same questions about my life and my future, I had no answers. I didn't travel at all for months, I stayed close to my bed, I rehired my therapist. Shifts in my financial security have always provoked self-doubt. And self-doubt is a bewilderingly intoxicating drug. It is easy for me to trust myself with my pleasure. I struggle to trust myself to provide a stable foundation of support. My instincts were honed for unstable environments, shifting circumstances, they are finely tuned to the immediate. Long-term, life-supporting plans feel like white-out condition snowstorms to me. Cancel school, close the roads, go back under a pile of warm blankets and hide from the whole world, indefinitely. I could feel the seduction of helplessness, I could hear it when I talked to my therapist. I already knew how to break the spell. To build a new trust took the same old skills. Take action, a small risk, move. I asked Sarah if I could come and visit her in India for my birthday that April. After we decided to visit the Himalayas, she sent me a list of possible activities. I picked a hike.

"What is my role here, if they try and stop you? I want to advocate for you, but I don't want to speak for you," Sarah said over breakfast at the Marriott we were staying in Mussoorie. Our mountain guides were on their way to pick us up.

"We have to wait and see. It's possible I can't actually do it," I shrugged. "But they won't know that, and I can't say for sure until I see it and try. My trick is to make a display of my skill right away. If they have the right spirit, that'll be enough."

In preparation for the winding roads to our starting point, we popped the anti-nausea pills Sarah had brought and a stick of mint gum.

When the van parked, I hopped out and pulled my chair over a rough hedge to the start of the path, popped on my modular hiking wheel that gives me extra leverage on uneven terrain, and headed down. Sarah and the two guides scrambled to catch up with me.

After several kilometres of up and down and over bumpy ground and giant rocks and narrow passes, Manish, the main guide, had the hang of it. I had taught him where to stand and how to brace against me when I used him as a guard rail between my wheelchair and the cliff side, pressing into his arm while maneuvering my wheelchair over rocks. He stopped to tell us about a saying in India, "Wise men don't make history; mad ones do." His eyes were full of the thrill of what we were doing. He was bouncing on the spot as he proclaimed, "We're the mad ones!," and then he pulled down a branch heavy with rhododendron and taught me how to eat the sour petals.

I asked Sarah to film cool parts of me making progress, showing her where to stand and what to get in the frame. When we got to the top, the last dozen metres of path were too steep for wheeling, so I hopped out, left the chair to Manish, and crawled up to the temple at the 2,200-metre-high summit.

He pulled juice boxes and snacks out of his backpack, and while we refuelled, he unfolded his map of the mountains in the area and pointed to the highest peak. "The next time you come, I will take you here."

It rained on the way back, my hands slipping on my rims, Manish's feet slipping on the soil. We put our heads down, drops pelting our ponchos. We were exhausted and dredging the bottom of our determination. We worked our way up to the car as one beast. We stopped outside a tea shop and our guides went to order us sweet and milky chai with extra ginger. Noting the dramatic shift in their demeanours from the morning, when they were quiet and serious, to the talkative and bouncy company we had now, Sarah commented that it seemed they had not expected to have such an adventure today.

I smirked. "They probably expected to leave me in the parking lot while you went and hiked. That's why there are two of them."

Sarah shifted in the back seat next to me. "Okay, yeah, actually, that's exactly what they told me this morning. I didn't want to say anything. I wasn't sure if it would upset you."

I shrugged. "I appreciate that. I love how mama bear you are. It makes me feel like I can go for it, and if something happens, you can handle it with me. But I've heard it all before. It's easier for me to figure out what to do when I know where people are coming from. Although, by now, I can usually guess."

"No more secrets," she promised. The guides soon returned with our steamy chai, and the warm tea soothed the aching chill in my fingers from gripping the slick metal of my rims in the Himalayan rain.

The drive from Delhi to Mussoorie and back gave Sarah and me hours to talk about our writing projects. I was writing my mini multimedia memoir, *Love All the Way*. I had just gone through a huge revision. I was still glowing from the love itself and extra-glowing from the satisfaction of capturing that love in words.

"The way I feel about him, and the focus it takes to write about what happened, having him on my mind all the time, with the way he involves himself, wanting to read all of it and comment on it, it feels like we're something, like we're together," I explained to Sarah.

"I totally understand," Sarah said. "He must really love you and trust you to let you do this."

"But he doesn't think of us as a couple, and that scares me."

I didn't need dating advice; I needed someone who understood how writing made the risk of a broken heart worth it. My feelings were simple: I was in love. And I loved being in love. But I also felt cautious about publicly declaring I was in love with someone who didn't want to be with me. I was still embarrassed by my romantic naivety, but I was choosing to expose it.

After you take enough risks, you get a feel for their rhythm, you get an instinct for anticipating what could go wrong. It's not the same as a blanket worry that something *will* go wrong, it's more like a series of scenes you play out, intuitively if not fully consciously, checking how each one feels and what your options for responses would be. You ask yourself *how would I handle this* and *what overall effect might it have on my experience?* This is how you calculate your capacity to handle the highest-intensity outcome. This is how you ask yourself *is it worth it?* It is also how you might come to overthinking.

"I feel like at some point, there'll be a reckoning for me," I said. It was somewhat comforting to know that when I wasn't a writer in command of her narrative and I was just a woman with a broken heart, I would have a friend who understood why I had put myself in that situation. Except I'd still have a broken heart.

The next day, the day before my birthday, we visited the temple at the site of the first home of the Dalai Lama after his exile from Tibet. There was a gold Buddha statue at the top of the hike, but this one had a railing. I left my wheelchair in the company of a couple ladies and pulled myself up the path, arm over arm.

A man outside the temple asked if I knew meditation. As I watched my feet for where they landed on the ground, waited for my balance to reset, pulled myself ahead, I thought of all the styles of meditation I had learned over the years. All the ways to do things slower and more consciously than they are usually done. Which is what my disability suggests I do as well. Be mindful of my body in every environment, every situation. Not to control it – I *have* no control over my body – but I could pay attention to how my body and life interrelated. In Buddhist traditions of meditation, there is a practice of dedicating the merit – the goodness – of the session to all beings.

The sitter (the person meditating) doesn't necessarily know what the merit *is* or *who* it might benefit, but they identify their practice as an act of service, a contribution to the wellness and happiness of all beings. Whatever merit there was in my slow ascent to the shrine, my slow ascent in love, I dedicated it to all beings. I could feel my steps in the burn in my forearms. I listened to the prayer flags flick the wind. All my focus was on the path up, the path down. My nose was running, and I sniffed hard. "My snot tastes like feelings," I said to Sarah, who was slow-walking with me, appreciating the shift in her natural pace and the view. "Like the sea. I am so grateful. This is actually happening. I am here. Happy birthday to me."

CHAPTER NINETEEN

A Good Girl
Algodonales, Spain, May 2018

My wheelchair was ready to fly.

And I was ready for my fourth paragliding course. The night before I left Vila Seca for Algodonales, my brother Ryan messaged me on Facebook: "Foxy was sluggish this morning. She threw up her breakfast. Mom is saying now she's having trouble breathing and her back legs don't work. The vet is doing an ultrasound."

"I'm reading. I don't know what to say. Keep me updated. I'm coming home in August. I hope she can hold on," I messaged back.

Elliott told me as we were divorcing that the only thing he'd warn someone about me is that I leave. The good things are true, I am as I seem, but I leave. He was right. I was leaving him when he said it. I left Foxy too.

Foxy was a Belgian Malinois – husky-border collie mix. She had crimped hair around her ears, and red, black, and beige colouring with white spots on her paws. Her tail was voluptuous. It curled up, and her hair was long and also crimped so it flowed in the wind when she ran.

There was a time when she came with me everywhere. She had full service-dog privileges. Restaurants, cafés, trains, planes, and scrunched on the floor at my feet in cars. She learned her commands in full sentences complete with Canadian politesse. *Please, thank you, excuse me.* But mostly we communicated in glances, expressions, and body language. On our best days, we were one vibe. One hair-tossing, sassy, tail-swishing vibe. We'd flirt with all the cute boys and girls everywhere we went.

When I took a meditation course, she was in class with me, quietly army-crawling under the chairs as we meditated as a class, asserting both her obedience and her autonomy. Even when she was freaking out, on escalators or boats, she trusted me. She waited out her panic, eyes on me the whole time. We moved to Salt Spring Island together, then to New York. When we rescued a kitten who had raging seizures and peed all over himself, she'd lie next to Peekay (as I named him) after I'd rinsed him off and lick him tenderly while he recovered. She was always up for an adventure. She was always up for selfies. She would hook her paw over my front wheels. She'd rest her chin across my back wheels and rock my whole chair with her exhale.

And then I left her. I told myself I could visit whenever I wanted. She'd be there when it was time for me to come home.

"Internal bleeding. Can you call mom? The vet wants to explain." My brother texted me.

It was 2 a.m. In a few hours, I would catch a train to the airport to fly to Algodonales to fly the wheelchair Luisma had made for me, for the first time.

I called my mom through Facebook messenger video. The emergency room vet gave me a bleak prognosis. Surgery was unlikely to improve things; even if Foxy survived, the recovery would be long and hard.

"Do the surgery," I said.

The vet's eyes bugged out. "Really? Most people in this situation don't make that choice."

What situation? Being thousands of miles away, desperately wanting to tangle my fingers in the crimped hair around Foxy's ears? Hearing her panting heavily, seeing her struggling to breathe through the screen on my phone, having to choose. Now. Making a decision I knew my mom would have to live with?

"Okay. Okay." I choked out a conflicted consent.

"I'll call you back, Erin," my mom said, meaning I didn't have to watch.

"No! Keep me with her. I stay!" I cried. "Let me see her." My mom reversed the camera so I could see Foxy. I was crying so hard that the bones of my face hurt. "I'm so sorry, Foxy. I love you," I said. "Hey, hey, it's okay." I repeated. And then she was gone.

"I got her to thirteen," my mom said. "I did a good job, right?"

All the resentment I had carried for the ways I believed my mom had let me down pressed to be let out. Would it have been different if I had been there? We were both asking this question. But, in the end, what did it matter? She had been there. She had rushed Foxy to the vet after two years of being her best friend, holding up her responsibility to Foxy and the primacy of my love for her. I had left, and my mom had been there.

"Yes. You did a good job, mom. Thank you." And then I added, "I wasn't there," repeating it over and over. We hung up.

I had paid Ryan to walk Foxy every day when my mom was at work. His income was low and the extra dollars were helpful. I worried about him after Foxy died and offered to keep paying him, anyway.

"That's okay," he said. "I'll just budget more carefully. I also want to say thank you. It gave me a lot of perspective to walk Foxy for that amount of time. It taught me that I can commit to something other than myself, an important lesson she helped you teach me. I can be responsible even when I don't want to be. It helped me work on patience. I am incredibly proud of how trusting you were of me. Foxy taught me more about real life than I ever could have guessed. There is no dollar amount on that. She will be with me for life."

I arrived in Algodonales the afternoon after Foxy died with a raging headache from crying and set about trying to socialize with a fresh batch of pilots. And I was still in love. I was nearing the end of the biggest writing project I had ever done, and the feedback other writers were giving my words glowed as deeply as I did for Mau. I was proud of myself. My heart ached for Foxy, and I felt the distance between me and every person I loved acutely. I was restless to know when I would see Mau again, every possibility he had tossed out had come and gone with no plan to see each other. I was also as high on altitude and happiness as a paragliding pilot could be.

The "para" in paraglide has nothing to do with being disabled. Unless you consider that all paragliding pilots are disabled birds. We scan the skies for vultures who have the mysterious and natural ability to detect thermals. When we see them flying in upward spirals, we know where the thermal air is. Paragliding is a controlled fall from the sky, and a thermal is a column of warm and rising air that will lift you so you can fly higher and, therefore, for longer – important for pilots who lack the ability to flap, like a vulture. No matter how much experience a pilot has, they are forever reliant on their harness and glider and technology to adapt flight to their limited, earth-bound bodies.

"It's so emotional for me to see you fly," a pilot said to me once. "I have this sense of awe seeing you..." his voice trailed off. "I have this idea, I think we all do, that, well, you're in a wheelchair, so you wouldn't be here flying."

I understood his sense of awe, but I didn't agree that it was because of me. "My takeoff isn't fundamentally more meaningful than your own."

People see my wheelchair and invent limits that they project onto me, then they are impressed by my ability to overcome limits that never existed in the first place. Flying is really awe-inspiring. For all of us.

José told me about the very first years of paragliding in this area, more than twenty years ago, when they flew with flimsy airfoils and took off from tiny patches full of rocks. Over time the launching sites got widened, cleared out. They found smoother and bigger landing zones; the technology of the wings improved and became more reliable and safer. But it started with passionate guys recklessly hurling themselves into the wind and learning on the way down. Their pioneering and perseverance was intrepid. To some, my wheelchair seems so innately tragic that my efforts are not intrepid but futile. It's inspiring that I persevere against futility. I will still be disabled when I land. But all pilots will be wingless, forever – no matter how advanced paragliding technology becomes, feathered appendages will never spontaneously grow from shoulder blades. Why is one adaptation adventurous and one sad? I think they are both a mix of each. There is something forlorn and unsatiated about all adventure.

What is inspiration for? I get called an inspiration like it's something I can be, an in breath, a reflex, a seizing of air. Being called an inspiration feels like being held at a great distance while people tell me how close they feel to me. Like they are trying to stroke a sunbeam – and I am the beam and so can't really be stroked. It feels like being as invisible as air, which you can only see when it moves something other than itself. The force of spirit can inhabit any of us, use us to move others, but then it stills, it goes elsewhere, and we are just humans again. As an inspiration, I am never just human to the people who see me that way, never just tiny, exhausted flesh. I am in a state of perpetual transcendence. And I think they see me this way because they are afraid. Bodies fail, weaken, are easily overwhelmed by the unrelenting steamrolling of the emotional content of life. I am a reminder of the worst that can happen – worse than death, life with physical impairment. So, seeing me accomplish things creates a visceral friction. Now I am also a vision of the best part of the human spirit – the triumph over limits. Because the human psyche has so often equated physical limits and their hardships with metaphysical, emotional and spiritual death, people who appear to defy their disability appear, metaphorically speaking, to be defying death itself. At least, that's how the fervour people express over the inspiration of disabled people strikes me when I see it. But death cannot be triumphed over. What an exhausting, tyrannical pursuit. Death will come eventually; all you can do is be at peace now. All you must do is the next small bit of living.

Inspiration is what reminds me to just keep going. Refocuses me, refuels me, gives me a soft boost, a bit of lift, a moment of play where there was previously a battle. Inspiration is something you can provide, not something you are. It's everywhere and we can all grasp it and pass it around like spiritual CPR, breath of life. When you are inspired, you rise up, you act. And those actions are contagious. We breathe together. We conspire.

Another pilot and I once joked that paragliding is the dorkiest sport. When pilots run for a takeoff, the part of the harness they will sit in once they're airborne hangs loose down the back of their legs and flaps awkwardly against their backside as they run, chest tilted forward, arms out behind them like children pretending to fly. Their legs paddle fiercely against the pull of the wing in a strong wind. It looks ridiculous. I have seen videos of pilots with such precise and elegant control over their wings that they remind me of my relationship with my chair. But most pilots flap and jostle and do okay. They will never be as acquainted with their adapted flying equipment as I am with my everyday chair. When we get in the air, it's not that I am like everyone else, it's that *they* are more like *me*.

The first few days of the course, José was hesitant about the flying wheelchair.

"I had such a hard time landing it, Erin. It tips over so easily, not like the buggy, which is more stable," he cautioned.

"Yes, yes," I said. "But that is a natural thing for me to handle, I'm balancing my wheelchair all the time, you only tried while landing. I'll be fine."

But then the wheat was too high in the landing fields, the wind too low or too fast. I was sure I could handle it, José wasn't, and this kind of risk takes a confident team. If his instructions and my responses didn't jive, all the disasters he was imagining could manifest. He wasn't wrong to be cautious, but neither was I wrong to be ready. We just couldn't take the leap together.

I needed Javi.

He joined us on the second week, and over lunch I begged him. "Please fight José for me, please! I know I can land the wheelchair in these conditions. I'm so scared of flying that if I'm confident, you know I really mean it!"

"I believe you," Javi said, not needing any convincing. "You will land with us today."

At the landing site, we debriefed on the plan, the backup plan, and the last-ditch landing avoiding any actual ditches. What worked between me and Javi wasn't that we knew what would happen and how we'd get out of it – actually, we had no idea. But we trusted each other to work it out no matter what situation we ended up in.

And so, I flew.

From the ground, Javi oriented me in the wind and watched me handle the bumps and gusts that rock the chair side to side and back and forth under the wing. I held steady and headed straight for him standing in the waist-high grass, dotted with poppies. My left wheel touched first – the exact thing that toppled José over. I shifted my body weight against the still-taut risers, bringing my right wheel down as the tension went slack and my front wheel hit the ground, my glider falling like silks behind me. Like a gymnast on a beam after a flip. Swaying slightly, straightening, perfect 10.

"That's my girl," Javi beamed.

Later, when, just as José feared, I landed in the middle of a field full of five-foot-tall wheat, I chucked my glider on the seat of my wheelchair, grabbed the frame and used the wheelchair like a walker, the giant monster-truck wheels plowing a path through the wheat. Javi and another pilot caught up with me. The other pilot took my wing for me, and Javi walked with me.

"I knew from all your other adventures that you'd know some way of getting out of the field if it happened," Javi said, amused by my method.

If I got tired of walking, I would at least make progress before I needed help, and in this way the effort felt more distributed between us. Javi was a firefighter, I knew if I ever needed an actual rescue, he'd have the right mind and physical strength for it.

But since I didn't need a rescue or help that day and neither of us minded the extra effort, we sang and joked on our way back to the pack of pilots, laughing at how fun paragliding in a wheelchair is.

Before the course ended, José had lunch with Luisma and I, and he detailed what had been on his mind since the wheelchair had been built. "If you want to get good at flying, for sure you should move here. If you decide to do it, we will help you with whatever you need to make it work for you. But I think this is your best option if you want to improve as a pilot."

I wanted to be a good pilot. I was all in.

CHAPTER TWENTY

Devotion
Algodonales, Spain, August 2018

The summers are hot in Algodonales. Stifling and airless. My apartment had no air conditioning, though at least it had a fan. This made it possible to sleep but not continuously. I was tired and sluggish, and no one was in town.

August is also the off-season for flying. The air is too hot to fly in the day, so the best chance you get is at dusk, and that's when company pilots do tandem flights. The school doesn't run any courses, so the instructors go on holiday. José wasn't even in town – he was in France, where he lives with his family when not teaching students how to fly.

The week before the first courses started, José arranged for Javi's girlfriend, Regina – an English teacher – to host a series of English classes to improve the instructors' grammar. Luisma, Pablo, Ivan, and Javi were the official students, but everyone was still on vacation, so several girlfriends also joined in. As did I.

During the lunch break of one of the classes, I started to feel so nauseated and dizzy that I left the restaurant before my food arrived and went home. I arrived in time to take off all my clothes and hug the cool tile of the bathroom floor before I became so dizzy that I couldn't lift my head or move. My stomach wasn't upset; I just had sudden, extreme vertigo.

I've been nauseated like this before, so my plan was to wait it out. But after a couple of hours, I was dying of thirst and couldn't raise my head enough to get water out of the tap. When Regina, who I'd been having lunch with, checked in with me, I asked her to bring me a bottle of water.

"I'm totally naked. Would you prefer I get dressed before you arrive?," I texted.

"I'm German, we love nudity," she replied. She showed up a few moments later with a huge jug of water, took one look at me, and quickly became profoundly concerned. "Erin, this looks bad. Are you sure you don't want to go to the hospital?"

We worked together to get clothes onto me, thinking we'd see if she could wheel me to the clinic. But two seconds of motion in the chair, and I dove for the floor in an agony of spinning and panting and puking.

José found out I was sick through a text grapevine and was coordinating with Regina about getting me to the hospital. Her own worry for me was swiftly rising after our failed attempt to get there ourselves. José called the hospital from France. First he sent an ambulance, but the driver didn't seem to understand the situation. I didn't lift my head when he arrived, but I was vaguely paying attention to the conversation. How did an ambulance driver not understand how to assess the situation? Was he only responsible for transport? That didn't make any sense.

I must have the Spanish wrong. I tried to lift my head up to see where I was at, and heaved a tiny pile of lettuce.

"What a beautiful pile of vomit," Regina cooed. We both hoped it would alleviate the vertigo. But the relief was brief. And I was back to pressing my check against the tiles for relief from the press of heat.

Regina updated José, who called the clinic again and had someone send the doctor to my house.

My bathroom was accessible from my kitchen at the back of my house, and it was filling up with the guys as they got back to town after an afternoon of flying. They had been kept up to date through the WhatsApp group and came to see how I was doing. By the time the doctor arrived with a nurse, my kitchen was full. Luisma, Pablo, Ivan, Javi, Regina, the ambulance driver, a doctor, and a nurse.

I was still lying on the floor, the world spinning so violently I couldn't risk a deep breath. I shallowly whispered answers to questions for Javi to translate without lifting my head. As I mentioned before, Javi is not just a paragliding instructor and my landing cheerleader, he is also an active firefighter teaching people to paraglide on his weeks off from saving people. He had the focused calm of someone used to emergencies. I am also used to emergencies. Communicating with Javi about my symptoms was efficient and soothing. However, it made more apparent the rudeness of the doctor.

"Perhaps she is dizzy because she hasn't eaten anything," the doctor offered dismissively while watching me panting and writhing weakly on the floor.

"I didn't pass out; I got vertigo," I clarified.

"Yes, but has she eaten anything?" The doctor insisted.

"She can't eat!" A chorus rose from everyone else in the room.

The nurse checked my blood sugar. Normal. The doctor requested that no matter how bad it got, I should not bother her at the clinic in the middle of the night: "I'm looking forward to a quiet night." She instructed the nurse on the treatment while all my friends stood around. "I think this is an unusual presentation of a gastrointestinal virus. We'll give her a shot in the ass to treat the vertigo." She actually used the Spanish word for word *ass*.

The nurse spoke to me so I knew she was behind me. Javi took my hand when I told him needles made me nervous. When I started to breathe too heavily, he talked me through a slower breath, and the nurse gave me a needle in a part of my "ass" I couldn't even feel.

"Oh, it's fine. I can't even feel it," I sighed, releasing my tension.

The mean doctor, the sweet nurse, and the useless ambulance driver left. One by one, the guys left. Pablo and Ivan, then Luisma, who had wedged himself in the corner sitting on the floor. Javi stayed to watch how the drugs took effect. He and Regina made plans to take turns staying with me so they could each bathe, eat, bring me food. Specifically, the noodle soup with breadcrumbs and garlic. Javi packed a fireman's overnight bag and spent the night in my guest room in case I needed anything.

The next afternoon, I woke up to my cat Peekay growling. He was curled up against my side, his paw possessively laid across my chest. Just then I heard footsteps approaching my open door, and Javi appeared. Again, Peekay growled – which was not something this loving, easygoing cat usually did.

Javi chuckled from the doorway. "I understand, Peekay. You have been taking good care of her, too." Javi told me Peekay had been sleeping with me every time he had come to check on me.

"You were here before?" I asked Javi, surprised. Partly because I hadn't heard anything, partly because it was a thorough act of care.

"Yes, Regina and I came several times today," he confirmed like it was no big deal – of course they had checked and were so glad I was feeling better.

It was a rather dramatic welcome party and a jolting start to the flying season, but it was inimitable in its sincerity. They would take care of me. They had promised that if I took the risk and made the effort to move to Algodonales, they would take care of me. Whatever I needed.

CHAPTER TWENTY-ONE

I'll Be More Like You
Algodonales, Spain, August 2018

Practising wing control without flying is calling kiting. Kiting lets you practise your sense of input. You learn how much pressure to apply to the controls in response to the constantly changing wind: too much brake pressure and the wing won't fly; too little, and you have no control. The wind pushes your wing all over, and your job is to keep it exactly overhead. Other pilots hop around to adjust left and right. I have to correct the wing before it goes too far to the left or the right to need to hop. In kiting exercises, you see pilots skipping and running all over the place to keep their wing balanced above their head. I stay perfectly still and learn to anticipate.

But first, the wing must inflate, and that means running. Since I'm using my hands to inflate the glider, I can't use them to push my wheels so, for me, "running" means Luisma pushes me. That meant that before he installed push handles, he was bent in half over the back of my chair, grabbing the backrest with enough force to give me thrust but making sure not to push down (which would make my chair crash backward to the ground), all while skipping over rocks and ruts and avoiding mud patches. I spent every last drop of energy Luisma had practising takeoffs. He barely complained. He wouldn't quit before I did.

I loved my instructors and my fellow pilots, but I wanted to hang out with them, not depend on them. It frustrated me that I needed Luisma to ruin his back and twist his ankles and strain his shoulders just so I could practise. And by "frustrated," what I mean is that I also worried that it was too much. Too much energy to ask of one person to pour into me so that I could do something for which I would very much like to take all the credit.

When independence is expected of you, there is the illusion that your activities are a relatively simple matter of either doing or not doing something. For me, once I have decided to do something, there is also the question of how involved other people will be. Some adaptations require help, and once you are being helped, the experience also belongs to someone else. When disabled people are facilitated, almost *all* of their experience belongs to the people who help them have it. The story is told by the volunteers, the meaning is shaped by the spectators, the scope of the experience itself is structured by a program, or by the limits of the imagination of other people, and not by the drive of the disabled person herself. The person with the disability at the centre of it rarely has a voice.

This happens in banal ways, too. Once, I dashed into my regular grocery store with a friend to pick up some last-minute items for lunch. The check-out lady who saw me there several times a week – always on my own – noticed my friend and said, "Oh, you brought a helper today."

"Actually, we're lovers," I said dramatically and swifted away before she could respond. The check-out lady could only imagine me in one kind of relationship. Someone paid to help me. The idea that someone might be with me for the pleasure of it wasn't an option. I had to make a special effort to keep messages like that from getting too close to my heart.

Some days the wind died in the middle of our field exercises, and we waited for hours for it to pick up again. Luisma would sit on one of my giant tires and show me cartoons on his phone, or he'd wander around looking for dried wheat stalks, for no reason other than we spent a lot of time sitting around doing whatever it took to entertain each other.

One day, he presented me with a hollowed-out stick with another stick inside it during a particularly dead-wind day. He demonstrated how the stick slid inside the other one. It was a strange offering – much like a cat bringing me a dead mouse, which could be a gesture of affection, or a meal. The cat knew what it meant, but it was bemusing to me. What was I supposed to do with a stick inside of another stick?

I gave him a quizzical look. "Thanks?"

"Do you see any sticks inside other sticks in this field full of sticks?" he asked me.

I looked around. "No."

"There you go, it's special," he said as he handed it to me.

It's a popular spectator sport at Levante, our home mountain, to watch pilots make early errors, jumping into their harness too soon, pulling too much on the controls or not enough, or correcting their direction in a crosswind too harshly with the ground so close. The game is to accurately call who will recover and who will be retrieved from the trees.

Walking pilots can abort. On a wonky takeoff, if they don't feel good about it, they can plant their feet or let their body weight in their harness anchor them to the ground and thereby kill their glider. They might be in the trees, but they are down.

On wheels, though, takeoff is all or nothing. Even if I kill the glider, if I'm on a slope I will keep rolling, picking up speed but not necessarily flying. Other pilots have to relax their minds and trust themselves and their glider despite the heart-pounding adrenaline induced by every takeoff. I have to trust all that and Luisma. I have to trust that while he's running downhill toward the edge of a 600-metre-high mountaintop, we're on the same page about whether or not he should let go.

We set up in the takeoff spot and watched the windsock for the right moment – the wind in the right direction, blowing directly into our faces.

My glider rustled in readiness. I pulled on the risers in my hands and it wooshed to life, rising up behind me, pulling my arms back with the force of it, the muscles of my chest and shoulders stretched and contracting to pull it up above my head, where it would settle into the sky and rise, lifting me up. Luisma braced my chair in place so I had something to press against.

We had a light wind. A light wind means you have to run more to get enough wind pressure under your wing. A light wind means you have to fight for the flight, drawing on all those afternoons spent running around Andalusian fields full of sticks.

Luisma ran.

The wing was still slightly behind my head when we reached our point of no return, before the slow gradient dotted with thistle bushes. The wing needs to be directly above my head to fly, the lines need to be tight, tight enough to cut through a couple layers of skin. But we didn't have that kind of tension, so Luisma started to pull back on my chair to kill the speed from our run and from the slope onto which we had just tipped. I started to pull in the brake lines to kill the glider, and like this we rolled and skidded until my front wheel hit a snag and spent the last of its forward momentum by flipping over itself and landing facedown.

My body hovered just above the ground, protected from impact by the frame of my wheelchair. I was still strapped to the chair by the harness. My limbs dangling, wheels spinning, pilots running to my rescue.

Everyone wanted to haul the chair backwards to set it on its wheels, but the pressure on my shoulders and thighs where the harness held me was too great.

"No. No! Don't pull. Unclip me!" I shouted, and hands reached for the clasps around my waist, each of my legs, and across my chest. I reached for the ground to catch myself, crumpling to my knees. Unscathed. I grabbed the frame of my upside-down wheelchair and spun around to see that Luisma's hand was still on the backrest of the chair. He had not let go, not for a second, the entire time. And he was panting.

But it wasn't his usual, out-of-breath pant.

"Are you okay?" everyone asked me.

"Are *you* ok?" I asked Luisma. He shook his head and looked down.

The back of his calf was bright red with blood. While I had been rolling and flipping, he had been dragged through the same thistles with no metal to protect him. The first layer of skin had been completely scraped off his leg.

But he hadn't let go.

I crawled back up the mountain slope. Luisma pushed my chair back up at a slow pace. We sat on the ground next to each other to catch our breath.

"Let's try again!" he said brightly. I shook my head. I was still processing what had happened to his leg.

Not trying again, not flying, meant we had to drive down the mountain, Luisma and me alone in the massive van meant for a pack of pilots and their massive gear. The road winds for about a half an hour. My eyes stung with road dust and tears. I squeezed my eyes closed and kept quiet, hoping Luisma wouldn't notice.

He noticed.

"Erin, don't worry. The wind was very light. You did very good. We'll try again tomorrow." He was thinking that I was upset about not getting the takeoff. Which was a fair assumption.

When I take off, all eyes are on me. And all cellphones. I'm representing the entire contingent of disabled people all over the world whose capacity to do anything is constantly underestimated and sentimentalized. This pressure to perform, to be actually and undeniably *good*, is so deeply internalized that I don't hear it as literal thoughts. It's a buzz under my skin that tickles or burns depending on whether or not I have appeased it.

The biggest job my coaches, teachers, and instructors generally have is calming me down when I am so tense with disappointment in myself that it burns.

But that's not why I was crying. The buzz was numb this afternoon.

"When other pilots take off, the only person whose life they're risking is their own. But when I take off, I'm risking yours, too," I hiccupped.

"You're crying for me?" Luisma said, surprised. He pulled the van over on the narrow road so he could hug me.

I cried harder into his shoulder.

Once I had pulled myself together, Luisma put the van in drive and shrugged. "Don't worry, Erin. I can just buy a new leg!" he declared triumphantly, picking up the tone of our usual banter. "Problem solved!"

We joked on the way down about how we were a team, and anyway how many working legs did we really need between us in order to fly. "One is enough," he said.

It occurred to me that Luisma had offered more than a joke to relax me into taking his risk in stride. More than just saying it was worth it. He was saying, "worst case, Erin, I'd just be more like you – and that wouldn't be so bad."

I didn't digest Luisma's nonchalance – or the danger of what we were doing – easily. I spent days telling the story to pilots in town. I was incredulous. Why would Luisma be so cavalier? It was obvious from his reaction to me that it wasn't a revelation to *him* that he was risking his life for this. But *why!?*

After offering generic comments about male pride and duty and the fulfilling heroics involved, a friend shrugged and said, "Erin, you just have to let him take his risk. Maybe it's about you, maybe it isn't. But it's his risk."

Weeks later, Luisma's parents visited Algodonales to watch him work. His mother fretted over everything. "He should take medication for that cough. He should put his jacket on. Couldn't he just go back to being a graphic designer like he studied to be and leave all this paragliding nonsense alone?

Wasn't he cold wearing shorts?" Looking worriedly at his bare legs, she noticed the red skin of his healing wound.

"Luisma! What happened to your leg?"

"That's my fault! I did that!" I told her while Luisma downplayed our dramatic story to his mother in Spanish. I was truly proud, though. His scarred leg was a sign of how much we trusted each other. And it reminded me of something we shared, something I valued in myself and respected in him: our risk-taking sensibility. His scar was also a sign that he should probably listen to his mother and wear pants when we flew.

CHAPTER TWENTY-TWO

An Homage To Something Real
Algodonales, Spain, September 2018

José joined us in Algodonales after I had already been there almost a month. I had completed and self-published *Love All the Way* and was exhilarated from reaching what felt like a new level as a writer while I was still getting used to my new limits in the city. As if he was breaking me out of confinement, José and I took a road trip to the big town nearby, with the box stores. He needed to buy a new laptop, I needed to buy a long-sleeved shirt as my stuff from Vila Seca hadn't arrived yet and the mornings could be chilly. We went for Chinese buffet.

When I had been in Bogotá with Mau, he had arranged a special, erotic photo shoot, separate from the movie scenes we recreated. The pictures were meant for us, but because the photographer was a professional artist, the idea of them being published and displayed was discussed.

In the middle of me eating greasy spring rolls with José, the erotic photographer texted to ask if it was okay if he posted some of the photos.

"It's okay with me. But you have to ask Mau," I texted.

"I already did," he replied with a smiley face.

"And he said it was okay?," I was dubious. Mau hadn't responded to me when I had texted him about it. He was at Disney World with his brothers, their wives and children, and various other extended family and wasn't reading my texts.

Without hearing from Mau, it *wasn't* okay with me if he posted them. I asked the erotic photographer which photos he was thinking of using and how he was planning to present them. The photos had not been his idea or created with his portfolio in mind. Technically they had been Mau's idea and he'd commissioned them. But if Mau consented, I could see it being interesting to have them out in the world.

I had given a lot of thought to how to present erotic imagery involving a wheelchair and an able-bodied lover. I texted the erotic photographer to make sure that he would mention that the images were a collaboration with me when he tagged me in them. I explained that I was concerned about the fetishization of an able-bodied man representing the sexuality of a disabled woman without providing proper context.

But even before there were blue double check marks indicating the messages in our chat had been read, the erotic photos had been posted to Instagram.

It was part of a series of collages the erotic photographer had made out of his other collections. Like a reconsidering of how his work went together. He was using the hashtag "come as you are." He chose a background of a natural Colombian landscape and positioned two photos from the same shoot over the background. I liked the idea, I liked his other posts from other shoots, but I did not like the post he had made of me.

There was one photo of me alone, naked, sitting a bit slumped in my chair. In the email of photos he had sent Mau, he had included a couple photos he had taken of just Mau but none he had taken of just me. I had never seen this photo. The photo he paired it with was one of me appearing to give Mau a blowjob. Mau's head is tilted back in simulated ecstasy, rendering his identity anonymous.

In the blowjob photo, you couldn't tell who either of us was. Using that photo on its own would have emphasized the wheelchair as the subject. With both of our identities obscured, who we were wouldn't be as important as the artistic statement about disability and sexuality in general. And arguably that was the photo to which the erotic photographer had the most exclusive artistic claim. He had posed us in that position. I would never have used that photo in my work, but I would have consented to it being used in his work. But paired with a photo of me alone, my face visible, something in the narrative shifted. Instead of an impersonal commentary on disability and sexuality, now it was personal but not completely personal. We weren't equally exposed and vulnerable. It wasn't a photo of two lovers. It was a photo of me performing a sex act.

I was distressed, and the language barrier made me tense. The photographer texted back a few emojis – a few hearts and a smiley face – that made me wonder whether he had understood what I had said. I wasn't going to be able to have a complicated conversation about fetishization and representation over WhatsApp. Maybe if Mau was involved, but he wasn't reading my messages either.

Meanwhile, there I was, eating Chinese food with José. I didn't want to show José the photos, and I didn't want to get into detail about my relationship with Mau, who had his own close relationship with José. However, my emotional discomfort was evident, so I asked José if he could help me compose a message in Spanish that asked the photographer to please not post any other photos he took of us that day.

He replied: [heart emoji, kiss emoji] "Yes, my darling. Tranquilo." I texted Mau to tell him how it had played out. He was still not reading messages.

As foreplay the night we consummated our physical relationship, Mau and I had taken selfies. Those photos were glamorous and light-hearted and sexy. I was wearing pearls and had my hair and makeup done from the *Rear Window* recreation we had just finished shooting. I was wearing a shirt of Mau's, and I started snapping photos as he started undoing the buttons.

The photos the photographer had taken the next day, after Mau had told me he couldn't let himself love all the way, were intimate and sad. We composed ourselves into the same positions we had been in the night before, inspired by ourselves. The direct comparisons between them told their own story, conveying the shifts in intimacy, the nuances. There was a photo with him standing behind my chair, his hand pressed flat over my heart and holding my other hand up in his, both of us staring directly at the camera, a mix of boldness and mournfulness on our faces. To me, the photo showed, no matter how complicated things might be, Mau would support me, show up, he would *be* there. But now, when the same series of photos were used without his permission and to my discomfort, where was he? Something didn't feel right, and, as was my usual reaction when something didn't feel right, I hungrily sought clarity. Why had Mau wanted to take the photos at all? Why did he risk them getting out and ruining his career? Alternatively, why did he encourage me or anyone to use them but then not participate at all in the process of them being used? I texted him long messages laying these questions out. My expectation was that if he understood why I needed these answers, he would find them in himself and give them to me so that I could relax. I thought of him watching me fight my distress when I needed his help to pee. "Just tell me what I can do or not do to make it easier," he'd said. He would ask me that question other times: "What do you need to relax?" But he wasn't asking me this time.

"HE ALREADY POSTED THEM???" Mau replied a week or so later.

He was sanguine about the photographer not getting his explicit permission. "The important thing, to me, is the fetishizing thing. Did you tell him how you felt?"

"Yes. I told him," I said. "I still felt violated." This was true, but it was not actually the biggest problem for me. Further violation had been solved rather swiftly and with José's help. The problem was that I was disappointed that Mau had not been part of that process directly.

"I understand," Mau said. "Did you show the photos to José?," He asked.

"No, I didn't show them to José." I didn't want to show them to anyone. I wanted Mau to tell me what they meant to him.

But maybe that was the point. I felt threatened by the pictures being out there, by the story being told the wrong way. Maybe for Mau, it wasn't the pictures themselves he needed to protect, but what they represented to him. He had told me so many stories in which revealing himself – who he really was and what he really wanted – had ended with him being rejected. The best way to stop people from using your own desires and vulnerabilities against you is to not share them. Hide them in plain sight. Let everyone think they know what they're looking at while you move among them, impenetrable. Maybe the exact thing that would make me feel secure and bold again, the specific assurances I needed to reconnect with him, were all a direct assault on Mau's defences. I could accept that, but it made me sad. It felt like there was no way back to the closeness I had felt with him.

Sanyu was my Instagram friend. I liked her posts on the origins of words and the Tao. Another writer, we could nerd out on words together and started having long, personal conversations in our DMs and then on WhatsApp. I'd been keeping her updated on my romantic life, so when the photos got posted, I knew Sanyu understood the intricate way my artistic sensibilities and personal feelings were intermixed.

A couple days later she sent me an email with the etymology from Etymonline for the word *fetish* and a musing of her own:

FETISH: "A material object regarded with awe as having mysterious powers or being the representative of a deity that may be worshipped through it," 1610s, *fatisso*, from Portuguese *feitiço*, "charm, sorcery, allurement," noun use of an adjective meaning "artificial."

The Portuguese adjective is from Latin *facticius*, "made by art, artificial," from *facere* "to make, do, produce" (from PIE root *dhe- "to set, put;" compare French *factice*, "artificial," restored from Old French *faitise*, from Latin *facticius*). Via the French word, Middle English had *fetis, fetice* (adj.), "cleverly made, neat, elegant" (of things), "handsome, pretty, neat" (of persons).

"Something artificial and in homage of something more real. Inspiration is what gets the ball rolling on this meaning. To produce, do, or make something because of being allured, because of art and because of being in awe of something. Thus, you set or put some production, some making, something you did forward. To externalize what for you is internal. And a fetish is always a reflection of the internal. Naturally, some fetishes are created better than others. More true to the thing or person or place they are honoring. More representative of what one claims to be representing. More transparent. Of more integrity. More encompassing. More genuine."

An homage to something real. That's what those photos had been for me. What was real in our selfies was our pleasure and happiness at being together and being naked. What was real in the photographer's photos was our pain, our vulnerability, still naked. We'd reclaimed the experience of being fetishized, objectified, flattened in meaning, and revived it with superstition, with a sense of awe.

In the photos the photographer had not chosen, the ones where you can see Mau's face, the look of devotion as he cradles my leg in his hand and brushes his lips tenderly against the inside of my knee are the perfect representation of something irrationally revered. One photo in particular, Mau holding me across his torso, my head tilted back in an unreadable expression of surrender or agony, reminded me of the Pieta. It was the *picture* of devotion, but what about its substance?

After the heat of the summer passed, paragliding courses started up again, and I joined a group of new pilots for dinner, where I was joking about my mom reading my freshly published opus, *Love All the Way*.

"It has sex bits in it, mom!," I had warned her over messenger when I sent her the link.

"Okay! I'll close my eyes when I read those parts," she had replied.

Relating the story at dinner enticed the table of new friends to ask about my piece.

I filled them in on the story I had written, and they started referring to Mau as my boyfriend.

"He's not my boyfriend," I firmly corrected them.

"Please tell me he knows about the essay!," one of them teased me.

"Of course he knows!" I sputtered. "He helped me write it, actually."

"He helped you write a graphic story about your relationship and then let you publish it? Sweety... he's your boyfriend," the pilot concluded.

That week, the inside joke was how none of them stood a chance with me against my movie-star-handsome boyfriend, who rode around in helicopters for his job and could also paraglide.

I loved it. The way they saw me. As a girlfriend. Wasn't that the whole driving force behind the photo shoot project in the first place? To recast a woman with a disability as the romantic heroine everyone envied or wanted to be with? Wasn't this the real-life proof we had accomplished our goal? It was, but I had also learned something about the emptiness of achieving the superficialities of love.

One of the rare times I remember being teased, especially as part of an ongoing campaign, was when I was in grade seven, and it wasn't even directed at me. Instead, I was the weapon. Classmates would start up a playful rivalry – hurling insults at each other until they'd reach a climax and whoever was next would say, "You like Erin!" Anyone listening would groan, "EW-WWWW!" and they'd all titter at each other. End of contest.

I never reacted. I pretended not to even hear it. I actually don't remember how it felt or what I thought, but I have always been reluctant to believe the teasing actually hurt or bothered me, being so nonsensical in retrospect. But now that I am a memoirist with the explicit job of making connections out of the fragments of my life, it seems meaningful enough that I remember it. I held on to that particular memory. Even if I had done what I could to let go of the humiliation it caused – or, more accurately, to not let myself feel anything in the first place. Still the memory would surface now and then; I would notice it the way I would a twig sticking up out of mud. I remembered twenty-six years later while sitting at a table full of pilots doing the exact opposite thing. They, too, were teasing each other and using me as the weapon. But now, I was "too good" and they "didn't stand a chance" and of course Mau was movie-star handsome and adventurous and cool. He'd have to be to have me. It was a point of obvious pride to have a crush on me.

❦

The first time I posted about us, with the series of romantic selfies we had taken when Mau visited, he asked me if people thought we were together. My first instinct was to apologize.

"Why do you feel bad?," he asked.

"No good reason," I said. But I did have a reason. I just hadn't connected it yet: "Because twelve-year-old Erin, frozen in time somewhere in my psyche, remembers that it is shameful to be romantically associated with me and she does not want to hurt you."

What my twelve-year-old self didn't know was that time would not just mature her, it would mature her age mates, too. She didn't know that this scene was playing out in countless classrooms with a staggering diversity of children as the weapon. Most of whom were not disabled. As cruel as it was, it was never personal. What my twelve-year-old self was grappling with wasn't mean classmates but the concept of self-esteem.

Self-esteem is based on an evaluation you make of yourself, but you gather the evidence with which you determine your worth based on evaluations others have made of you. One feeds into the other. A common theme in advice on building self-esteem focuses on achievement, on assessing your accomplishments, your strengths, your weaknesses. But how do you determine which achievements reflect your worth? What if all your weaknesses are visible and representational – symbolic of fundamental human weakness?

I represented a portion of society very low on being esteemed; disability brought and caused shame. The highest esteem a disabled person could receive was pity. It was never enough for me.

I was born with innate self-esteem, I had confidence right out of the womb. I liked myself very naturally. I liked life, I liked living it, and I liked being me. But that was not reflected in people's responses to me. Strangers routinely offered me and my mother condolences on my existence. Maybe I don't remember feeling rejected or hurt by my classmates' game because the pain was more existential. My heart was already broken. We were all grappling with our sense of worth, value, and belonging. We were pre-teens; that was our job. But I was forging the belief that I would have to spend a lot of my energy trying to exchange a mountainous pile of unearned shame for an equally unearned pride if I stood any chance at being happy.

I texted the story of the jealous pilots to Mau. He texted an elongated AWW, followed by some smiley and laughing faces; he was charmed by it. This clarified nothing for me. He made a comment about it being cool and then disappeared again.

Nevertheless, in that mystical way that healing can time-travel, a message made it back to twelve-year-old Erin sitting in Ms. Lowry's class, her head buried in a book hidden inside her desk, escaping into R.L. Stine fantasies instead of paying attention in class. "You will grow up to be very proud of who you are. One day, it will be a mark of good taste to have a crush on you, and you will care more about the integrity of the relationship." Now that twelve-year-old me knew that and could get through the next twenty-plus years, I could get started – in my late thirties, in love and frustrated – on understanding that it wasn't pride that replaced shame, it was connection.

My friends and internet acquaintances were now starting conversations with me by asking how Mau was, giving me the chance to gush and celebrate the new love in my life. They wanted an update. It was generous and it frustrated me. I could tell them all about his life, how work was going, where he was travelling, what he was hoping to do. Our conversations happened in unpredictable spurts, but I knew all those things. And that just made me feel like I needed to clarify: "You do know we're not together, right? He doesn't want to be together." Rejecting myself over and over was not the way I wanted to celebrate, but it was the only way I could figure to make the essay and the relationship feel honest.

It was the same feeling that had nagged me when he told me he didn't want to be together, but he did want me to go ahead and write all about it and post erotic photos of us. I was still fu-elled by determination. It wasn't that I didn't recognize the bar-riers and distance and complexities between us. But the magic of what we could be if we went for it was undeniable to me; it was so alive, it had its own pulse. If we both wanted it, we'd be an unstoppable force, which we could apply to anything we chose. And I had an idea of where we could start.

I told him: "Come with me to Namibia, let's write a movie."

I wanted the two of us out in the adventurous world, giv-ing our considerable combined energy to whatever we decided deserved it. He had a secret screenplay he had been working on. We had bonded in the first place by making a short video together the first week we met, pushing each other to make tighter edits, arguing over the sequencing of scenes, the excited chatter of ideas. Then there was the photoshoot, and that he'd been the first to joke that we were so good at collaborating, we should make a movie together. It was a bold request but not entirely unprecedented. I wanted us wild and creating.

I thought that was what he wanted too. He kept asking to collaborate with me. But when I shared a project with him, he ignored it. When I told him my idea of going to Namibia to-gether, he dismissed it. The cycle of asking to collaborate then rejecting me was so unlike the way we had approached the first film we made, all the writing projects between then and now, the photoshoot itself. Mau had always been inconsistent in his focus and timing, he'd always exasperated me, but projects had eventually progressed. Now there was a total stall, like I was misunderstanding what he meant by "collaborating."

"I figured with all the risks you have been willing to take for me to publish this story, I thought it had more weight."

"It does have weight," he replied. "I guess I'm just too much of a pussy or too motivated by my job right now to quit and be all entrepreneurial."

It seemed extravagantly defensive that in order for us to collaborate he had to entirely quit his job. An all-or-nothing strategy with a high probability of nothing.

After a couple weeks of silence, he texted to apologize for being so distant. It turns out, he had been dating someone. He was back in touch now that it was ending, he'd just been feeling really sensitive. He had never once mentioned dating someone. Not when I told him the boyfriend stories, not when we talked about creating art out of our erotic photos. Not a word until it was over.

"I thought we were closer than that," I fumed, expelling an inarticulate humiliation. I felt confused about what I was even asking for. More details about his romantic life and how I wasn't in it? No, but this was still something I should have known. We argued back and forth about the nature of our relationship.

"I think we have different expectations, and I don't know what to say," he said.

"I just realized we are not on the same page at all, and I don't know what to say either," I replied.

"What page are you on?," he asked.

How was that unclear to him? I had just published a massive digital memoir, which he had read several times, detailing the page I was on. I was thirty-three pages of publicly in love with him.

"I want us to be together. I want us to make more stories together," I said.

"I love collaborating with you, but what if someone else does come along? I am confident it wouldn't change anything about our relationship, but it would suck for me if you had a bad reaction. Maybe it's naive, but I think everybody can just get along," he said.

What *if* someone else came along? Someone already *had* come along. That was the whole point of this conversation. Someone had come along and changed *everything*. His newly ended relationship was the reason he'd been distant and non-committal during our conversations about collaboration. It *was* naive and infuriating. "Get along" on whose terms? He was basically saying we were friends with benefits, but instead of sex, he had the benefit of access to the interior of my creative process without giving me the benefit of his commitment to it. Maybe it didn't change anything he felt, but it changed *everything* for me.

"I think we need to be very careful about our expectations," Mau said finally.

Well, I had been trying to do exactly that, and I was still way off. How I was supposed to know what reasonable expectations were if he was withholding crucial information? Who was I to him? What did he want?

Most importantly, what did *I* want?

If I had known Mau couldn't let himself love all the way, I wonder if I would have slept with him. The photos would have meant something else, if they had happened at all. I didn't regret it, but it changed things. If I had known he was dating someone, I would have posted about us differently. I kept finding out about these factors afterwards, but they weren't unpredictable. If they changed things for me, then I couldn't wait for him to tell me where things stood for him. I had to decide where they stood for me.

Choosing to decide what things mean to me, imagining a life outside of the available options, has always freed me. It gives me the power to build my own life. To feel love where I had only known pain. I take my wheelchair all over the world; I make it fly. And I blew a romance out of proportion. It's all the same me, all the same force.

Meaning gives things weight, and it weighs things down. It can propel you forward or keep you stuck in place. There's no one formula for timing, or the precise amount of meaning to use in any situation, just a constant rebalancing, adjusting to every other force affecting you. Mau had said what happened between us was beautiful and special and the intimacy was deep and genuine. And the way I can weave meaning into things was some part of that. But it was also over. Not because we didn't love each other but because, despite every natural instinct screaming inside me, maybe you can't be determined for a place in someone else's heart.

It had been a romantic fantasy, for someone – Mau – to put up a fight, to not let me go. Having it happen in reality revealed the obvious flaw: What had created the need to fight for me in the first place? His own ambivalence. He created the abandonment, then enthusiastically reappeared to relieve me from it. He wasn't fighting for me, he was fighting with himself. I was just caught in the middle.

CHAPTER TWENTY-THREE

Before Death, French Fries
Algodonales, Spain, October 2018

I moved to Algodonales because I wanted to feel like a real pilot. I wanted my flights to belong to me. My instincts, my decisions, my actions. I wanted to take the last months before my Spanish visa expired and dedicate them to solo flight.

When I came for a week or two, the guys handled my glider on takeoff, guided me in for landings, instructed me mid-flight through the radio. I wasn't progressing, and the takeoffs were so complicated I didn't see a way to get there. So José advised me to move there. The idea was that if I was flying all the time, it would happen naturally. With less pressure.

But that is not how it panned out. I barely flew. The first month and a half I was there, I had one solo flight. The weather conditions weren't right, there wasn't enough room in the van. And I wasn't at the point where I could just toss my gear into any old van and ride up like any other pilot. I was there to learn to fly without my instructors, but I still *needed* my instructors to fly. I was getting nowhere.

José could see it, the way I was waiting as patiently as he'd asked me to. And I could feel it. Maybe I'd set the wrong goal for myself. What did it look like for me to be "good" at paragliding? What would progress look like? What does independence mean in a situation like this?

José decided we should add more ground handling. I and the very young and very new instructor, Ivan, could take gliders when we wanted and practise in the off hours, goofing around confidently. We'd drive out to the sunset-drenched Levante landing ground and leap around the sticks and stones, inventing takeoffs we would never use for an actual launch.

Maybe it was his youth, but Ivan understood it was important that I was doing it myself. That I had something to prove to myself about what I could do. Maybe he felt that way, too, because it was Ivan who invited me to fly with him. Not as a student but as friends driving to the top of a mountain and taking off. He *could* instruct me, but he wouldn't.

"Erin, you have to ask José. I don't think he'll say yes if I ask him," Ivan texted me. I wasn't sure José would say yes if I asked him, either. I honestly had no idea what his markers were for my experience level. They seemed to fluctuate with his anxiety levels. I felt ready, but did he agree?

When José gave the go-ahead, Ivan and I were giddy like teenagers scenting new freedom. We were going to be the ones who made this happen. And we were going to film it from every angle. We were prepared for uncontested glory.

The sunset at Ronda la Vieja had gilded us in gold. The grasses had given up their green, they were a flowing yellow sea as far as the eye could see. And from this height, we could see far. We were trophies in flight. The late afternoon is often a good time for gentle flights, the temperatures have evened out, the wind becomes steady after a day of gusting up the cliff.

Ivan's dad, a documentary filmmaker, brought his camera and filmed as I angled my chair into position on the slope, Ivan's foot against my front wheel to break it. I hooked into my harness, checked the lines. There was no team, no crowd of observers, Ivan was not there to instruct me, he was there to fly with me. The three of us had the whole mountain to ourselves and the lightness of that privacy brought me an ease I had never felt for any takeoff before. After two years of paragliding courses, making meagre progress, it was finally time.

Ivan held the back of my chair, waiting for my cue. I felt the breeze against my cheek, checked the direction it pushed the dying grasses, tugged my lines to feel the glider. There was no labour, the wind lifted me immediately from Ivan's grasp and my control kept my ascent steady. I slipped from his hands into flight. It was a triumph, my flawless takeoff.

Once I was airborne, Ivan took off. There would be no one on the ground to give me direction, I got to choose and I chose to play. We weaved and swooped around each other, I was giddy with success. Intoxicated with being a pilot freshly at ease in the air.

"Let's try and land at the house!," Ivan called out. "Follow me!"

We'd need height to make it all the way to the house by the road, and I was already a foot or so lower than Ivan. But if we had enough speed, it was still possible. I lifted my hands all the way up, releasing the breaks entirely, indulging in a surge of confidence as I flew past the familiar boundaries of our usual landing site.

"Erin, I don't think you are high enough. Let's go to land now." Ivan called out. "Go to land" is a shorthand for a series of calculations that I hadn't kept in my mind and as I turned back to the landing field and tried to track the wind direction to orient myself against it, my mind went blank.

There are several ways to tell which way the wind is blowing on the ground while you are in the air. Smoke, there was none. Grass or wheat or trees, the fields had been harvested. The dirt did not blow. Windsock, no. You can feel the direction on your face, the wind feels everywhere. You can look down and watch the ground move under you, if you are in line, you will move ahead straight, if the wind is pushing you from the side, you will move sideways. The ground is so close, it is rising up so fast. What direction is it rising from – smash!

Dragged. Scraped across the loam. Grounded. The front wheel from the chair Luisma made me, snapped.

Crash.

I bounced and skidded up the lumpy hill of the harvested wheat field. All around me lay the bare soil dried by the Spanish sun in rocky clumps with razor edges. Banging my arm, my ribs, scraping the skin of my shins as my paragliding wing dragged me, still harnessing the wind.

Ivan's shouting crackled at me over the radio.

I wanted to lie still, to pant, but I had to get to my radio and I was upside-down, pressed into the shoulder straps of my harness by gravity, the weight of my wheelchair preventing me from rolling easily or pushing upright. The radio was between my hip and the ground and I couldn't reach it. I had to undo the straps. My hands shook as I tried to squeeze the clips to release them. Each release increased the weight pressing into the other clips, making them harder to release. Finally I was free enough to reach my radio.

"I'm okay," I called out. I finished unclipping myself, more slowly. Crawled out from under my chair. Took a deep breath. *Was* I okay?

It was the kind of crash I had seen new pilots take in their first few weeks of flying, landing too hard, misjudging the wind direction, not flaring at the right time. They'd hit their butts hard or scrape the palms of their hands, then they'd learn and move on.

But I hadn't had the chance to make those mistakes until I'd had too much experience to justify miscalculating the wind direction. It was like being friends with someone for too long to suavely ask for their name.

I was burning with embarrassment. Was I even a pilot at all? My pride hurt, but my body had been shielded by my wheelchair.

When Ivan reached me, he asked me again, "Are you okay?"

I nodded, shaking and still a bit winded from shock. "Yeah. I'm fine."

"Before you moved, I thought you were dead." He exhaled, shaking visibly with his own shock. "Are you sure you're okay?" Ivan kept asking. He made me rotate my arms around in their shoulder sockets. I already couldn't stand, so we didn't check that. My arms ached, there would be massive, fig-coloured bruises by the next day. I took in slow, successively deeper breaths. My ribs hurt, but I could breathe. I patted myself down my sides and my torso and legs, feeling for tenderness lost in the shock. Nothing. I tilted my head side to side, all fine. The skin on my ankles was rubbed off from scrambling around in the sharp soil without having control or sensation of my feet. The blood soaked my socks, but it didn't hurt. I was okay.

"We have to tell José," said Ivan, sighing in resignation. Then I was not okay.

The thoughts running through my head coming down from the hill were harsh, sharper than the edges of the dried soil clumps scraping the skin off the parts of my ankles where I had no sensation.

"You have to be better than other pilots. You can't make mistakes like this. You know how to land! What were you thinking?," I was expecting an irrevocable chastisement. José and the other instructors had all invested so much extracurricular effort, time, and expense into me, and then I crashed. Broke the chair, didn't deserve so much, shouldn't have reached so high.

It wasn't only my risk. It had also been Ivan's. Would this mean he wasn't ready to instruct? Would Jose trust him less? It had also been José's risk. His reputation, his company. An able-bodied pilot could be a goof, make a dumb mistake, hurt himself, and everyone would shake their heads at him and move on. With me, if I got hurt, it would be someone else's fault. Regardless of whether it was true or fair, that was the fear. Other people taking too much responsibility (and therefore exerting too much control) over the things I did. This was why people so often said "no" to me. They were afraid that if something bad happened, it would be their fault. And not just legally. Not just as a liability. But morally. They would be blamed (or would blame themselves) for the injuries to the disabled girl.

My kindergarten principal was worried about this, Mrs. Loson and the school board were worried about this, the bus driver the night I met Elliott had been worried about this. How much bigger was José's right to also feel like this, when the risks were actually real.

Ivan texted Jose and I texted with Laura when I got back into the car. I was despondent, slumped against the car door. I was certain they would never let me fly again. She talked me down, texting: "You sound like a teenager who crashed her dad's car. You might be right that he might be disappointed in you, but you will get to drive the car again. It's probably good that you are contrite. It means you'll learn."

A text from José came through: "Are you okay?"

"Yes, but the chair is broken."

"Did you hit your head?"

"No. The chair took all the impact."

"It's okay. This is just something pilots have to deal with. Try not to worry too much. Perhaps we need to review approach and landing?"

"Yes. Please."

Aside from Ivan, who had actually seen me go down, no one was the least perturbed.

José and I had lunch together a couple weeks after my crash. The absolutely best chocolate cake was at La Cueva, and that's what I wanted.

"Quiero muerte," I told Antonio when I ordered. *I want death.* He had once told me the cake I loved was called Death by Chocolate, so that was how I always ordered it.

"Anything else, or just death?" He asked me.

"Antes de la muerte, patatas fritas," I said. *Before death, french fries.*

"José, do you want to see the film I made of my crash?" I asked.

I couldn't remember the details of what had just happened. What had I been trying to do that had ended in crashing up the slope of the hill? I knew how to land at Ronda la Vieja. Landing was my best and favourite skill.

Watching the video, I could see the mistakes. The main problem was that I landed in a tailwind, which was the opposite of how you are supposed to land. When you land into the wind, it creates resistance, it slows your landing down.

"Did you calculate the wind direction?" José asked. I re-watched the moment I should have turned to hold a straight line for my final approach. I do not turn. I was too close to the ground before I realized I was facing the wrong way. I had no more time to think it through.

Just before landing, at a very precise but intuited height, I must pull the brakes all the way down behind me. When executed at the exact right moment, it lifts me up slightly just before touching down so that I land as gently as a feather.

I was going in the wrong direction, and the ground was coming fast. At the moment before impact, instead of putting my arms down and behind me to soften the inevitable blow, I reached out for the ground.

I didn't flare.

"The flight was perfect! We are focusing too much on the crash," José insisted. "But I think it was good for you – to fly alone with Ivan, without us there to supervise. It's like you have to fly away from the nest."

I nodded.

"It took longer than we expected, but when I see this, I don't feel any of the emotion that, "Oh, Erin is flying," meaning the inspirational preciousness he knows I hate. "I'm more excited about the new handlebars on the chair. It makes it so much easier to control and run with you. But your takeoff was just normal," José said.

"It's true. It's not something we have to figure out anymore. We did it. We figured it out. It took us two years, but we really did it. Now I just need to practise it," I said, and then I shovelled another bite of death by chocolate into my mouth.

CHAPTER TWENTY-FOUR

Crashing Is Part of the Sport
Algodonales, Spain, October 2018

The scrapes on my ankles ended up infected. Whenever my body is fighting an infection, I get a bitter taste in the back of my throat. Often, especially if the infection is somewhere in my body that I can't see or feel, and before a fever sets in as the final warning sign, that taste is the only symptom I have. I needed my wounds disinfected, and I needed antibiotics, so Luisma drove me to the clinic one night after one of his typical long days instructing new pilots.

The body needs sensation to regrow strong and healthy skin. It takes longer and is a more tepid healing process when the wound has no sensation – when there is no sting of nerve endings to tell the brain to send its best resources to the site. Painlessness is not a blessing when healing is needed.

I spent the days I was healing and waiting for my chair to get repaired at La Cueva, the pizzeria in Algodonales run by Antonio and his father, also named Antonio. I worked on an adaptation from *Love All the Way* for a competition and grieved.

"Crashing is part of the sport," I was told nonchalantly, over and again, and I said it to Mau when he texted me on the day I crashed.

"That makes me think it's also a metaphor for love," Mau texted. And, in the midst of a long text: "I've been thinking a lot about what you said, and I don't see us ending up together."

"I am bruised all over. Also a metaphor for love," I wrote.

When I was sitting in those church services as a girl, along with my dream of playing the tambourine as well as the pastor's oldest daughter, I was also imagining how the Holy Spirit would bring me relief. If I held on to my faith in God, on very specific terms, for long enough, the Holy Spirit would pour through me and make my life easier. It would take away the stress and fear and flood me with peace. I was holding on, in the same way, to love. I had to be determined because I had mostly known love that was stressful, tense, terrifying, and dangerous. When you loved someone, that's what you committed to – managing the stress it caused. If you held on long enough, and if you got lucky, love would take over and make it easier, flood you with peace.

While I healed, the sky rained so hard and so uncharacter-istically that it wiped out parts of Ronda, a nearby town, and reminded me of the forces I had longed for as a girl in church. Torrents of spirit promising peace to a parched soul. But these torrents of rain did not bring peace. How would any torrent, really? They bring destruction. Always.

Algodonales residents passed around their cellphones, showing each other Facebook videos of the roads turned into white water. Some were funny, and some made us press our hands to our hearts in shock. José had to refund some courses. The region was renowned for paragliding because of the high ratio of flyable days, particularly in comparison to the UK, with their rainy, cloudy, miserable weekends. It is almost unheard of to send British people home from Spain to better weather, but it happened a few times at the end of that summer.

La Cueva had WiFi, and my apartment did not. Antonio the younger unplugged the gambling machine so I could plug in my laptop, brought me brownies from the bakery, and made me as much coffee as I could drink. I'd linger near the window for as much light as possible while he would tease me for eating french fries every day and let me sit there as long as I pleased. The essay won first prize. Two first-place wins for essays I had written about Mau and me.

I write like I love. I write *what* I love. My writing *is* my love.

Falling in love and feeling the inspiration for a story rush through me are the same feeling.

In every way, writing and love are intertwined.

I did not know this consciously about myself before I met Mau. Before I crafted and published the entire story of our re-lationship. I'd had and become the lover I'd dreamed for my-self with him. I expressed my love for him in words; I took his love in through touch. I thought those things would recipro-cate more evenly. Instead, his touch was what had made me feel loved; words were how I expressed the love I felt in return. His touch, my words, our collaboration of energy. I'd finally felt the way into my own sexuality, experienced a way my feelings and my lust connected. I knew a way in now. I had become the woman who could write the story.

What do you call the person who showed you something like that about yourself? Who loved you in a way that helped you become more of yourself? What do you call them after you can't share your intimate self, after you can't write *with* them anymore? How can someone like that be any kind of an ex? They are part of everything after.

I called Laura when I found out I won and sobbed into the phone, gasping for air. Something about my growing success as a writer, maybe clarity shaped by the contrast, finally forced me to feel the loss of my connection with Mau. Even though it had happened more than a year before, the day he told me exactly everything I needed to know about our relationship when he said, back in Bogotá, that he didn't want to be in one. "This doesn't mean more to you than it does to me, but I don't want to be in a long-distance relationship."

In the end, my ankles took two weeks to heal. My pilot friends entertained me with stories of their much worse, much stupider crashes. Trying to nudge me out of taking my own crash so seriously. My wheelchair was repaired and, in a break in the rainy weather, I flew again.

A couple of the pilots, Vern and Wouter, that were with me for my first flight post-crash had breakfast with me the next day.

"You will never fly alone," Wouter said. We were talking about my solo flight ambitions. Wouter was an experienced pilot, and while Vern was new to paragliding, he was previously a Red Devil parachuter. We were sitting at La Cueva, drinking tea and coffee and getting out of the rain. I was humbled by heartbreak and the literal healing in my body. I nodded my agreement with him.

"Do you fly alone?" I asked Wouter, and he nodded. "So you hike up?" I inquired, and he nodded again.

"Well, I 'hike' up," he said, sticking his thumb out, meaning he hitchhikes up to take off.

"I have seen wheelchairs take off unassisted, but they were on lovely, grassy, perfect slopes. Nothing like we deal with here," I said with a flicker of defiance. But my defiance was weak, and I wasn't sure in all my bruised humility if it was even my goal anymore.

Vern and Wouter complimented my takeoff from the day before.

I smiled to acknowledge the praise, then confessed: "It was my first flight since my crash," I said. "Two weeks ago."

"That's a lot of time to think about it." Vern crumpled his face sympathetically. "In the Red Devils, they'd come grab you and get you right back in the air after a bad flight so you couldn't think about it at all."

I didn't worry too much for the two weeks. I was too frustrated and humiliated over crashing. But after my flight yesterday I was incredibly sad," I said.

Luisma had been in the landing field, staying quiet, specifically not telling me the wind direction, watching me while I made my approach all on my own, landing at his feet. He closed the distance in a bounce ready for a hefty high-five, but when he saw my face, my brimming eyes, he sank to his knees to be eye level and tilted his head. "Emotional?," he asked, and I nodded and shrugged. He was quiet for a moment and then said, "It was a perfect landing!" And it had been. Without saying anything else, Luisma raced my chair wildly around the field until I giggled from the speed.

Back at La Cueva, I was still dissecting with Vern and Wouter. Antonio cleared our breakfast plates and brought me a refill of coffee with the tub of raw sugar I preferred from the kitchen supply. "I had a good takeoff. A good landing. And I handled both on my own. But I didn't feel triumphant. José asked me why I was so serious on takeoff, and I didn't know how to explain that I wanted to cry."

Whatever had been underground for the two weeks that I was waiting for my chair to be fixed and my skin to heal made it to the surface while I was flying so I could let it out. The "whatever" being the vulnerability of getting in the air again, the pressure to have a good flight, and Mau.

When we had been shooting *Casablanca,* I had been goofing around. Mau, on his knees, the collar of his jacket tucked up, wearing a fedora at a slight angle, was getting annoyed.

"No, Erin, come on. You're never going to see me... she's never going to see him again." He'd meant the characters were never again going to see each other again. He had wanted my eyes full of a graceful grief; I faked it. Because in real life, I was giddy from falling in love.

At that time, it didn't seem possible I'd never see him again. I had been fortified with faith in us. It felt like a beginning, not an end.

It felt possible now; it felt almost certain. If anyone took any photos at all of me on the landing field after my first post-crash flight, or on any day of the two weeks after that, or that morning having breakfast with Vern and Wouter, my eyes would have shown that noble but restrained sense of loss Mau had prodded me to affect during our *Casablanca* shoot. My eyes, my entire aura, now had the perfect ring of sorrow.

"You maybe need a female friend you can talk to," Vern said, with sincere concern. Evidently the depth of our conversation was making him feel inadequate to counsel me, though I felt perfectly supported as we talked.

"I just went home and sobbed for the afternoon," I shrugged. Meaning: *I handled it.*

"That's good," Wouter said. "We are like kettles full of water, and when something happens the water starts to boil and the pressure builds. The whistle is our tears. You need to let them out. I always say it's good to cry when you need to."

I didn't need a woman to talk to about my feelings. We were talking about them right now. And I can always talk about feelings with other pilots. Men and women (though mostly men) show up for a week or two; we bond intensely in the many hours a day we spend training and sitting around and flying together. We frequently debrief afterwards in bars and cafés, and our debriefs are as much about how we are feeling about our flights as the technical aspects of them.

"Paragliding has so many feelings for me," I mused. "Is it like that for you guys, too?"

"Mainly fear, for me," Vern admitted. He then shared a couple stories of parachuting recklessness in his youth, near death and total terror. "Have you ever experienced time slowing down?," he asked me.

"Yes. All the time," I said. "I have this thing where my senses separate and I can experience them individually. I can hear my mind chatter, I can see what my eyes are seeing, I can hear what my ears hear. All on separate tracks. Sometimes, I can kind of activate it."

Vern's eyes widened. "That sounds incredible! When it happens to me, I think of it as my superpower. I was in a fight once and everything slowed down. I could actually feel the vibration of the guy's fist in the wind as it passed my face. It was like *The Matrix*."

"It is like a superpower," I agreed. "And it's been incredible for my writing. But it also produces a lot of cortisol. I think it would be ultimately destructive to me if I wasn't getting so much therapy," I said with a laugh. "It can take a while for all my parts to coalesce again. It's been two weeks since my crash and I'm just starting to feel like I'm back together."

"For some people, it takes ages. Or it never happens," Wouter pointed out.

Crashing *is* part of the sport. Love, life, and paragliding.

The ground is unrelenting. We can leave it – and that's its own kind of shock, an elated rush of triumph. Flight is easy when it's beautiful. It's easy when it's washed in the calm, golden glow of sunsets, and our view is vast, and we are in the company of clouds and vultures and our friends who can also fly. But we must come back down. When the impact is ugly, demeaning, when it slows down time and splits your senses, you don't just have to come down, you have to come back together, and then you have to hike back up and take off again, now knowing more precisely what you risk.

CHAPTER TWENTY-FIVE

It Shows Somehow in the Eyes
London, Ontario, Canada, December 2018

I was spending the 2018 Christmas holidays with my mom and my two brothers when my grandmother, my mom's mom, started dying.

My mom had cleared out her office, set up the bed I had panic-bought after my divorce, along with all the other furniture she had held on to for me, and put out a pile of some of my books that had been stored in her closet.

"I thought you might appreciate seeing some of your books!" she said.

I hadn't seen a lot of my stuff since my divorce, four years before.

My Spanish visa had been approved on Christmas Day the year before, which meant that it also expired on Christmas Day. I was trying to find ways to make the ending feel like as much of a gift as the beginning had. I was going to do several months of travelling with a plan to return to Spain after the winter – this time as a tourist without a visa, temporarily – while I adjusted to the fact that I wouldn't be living there. Spain wasn't home anymore. I was floating between places, at home everywhere but not anchored to any place. Setting out my books, a material and tangible element of my sense of home, had been a surprisingly astute gesture of compassion by my mother.

After Christmas, just before I was set to leave on my next trip, my grandma took a final turn. She died slow and ugly. It started with Alzheimer's and ended in a week at the beginning of January with her gasping for air, unable to be given even a congealed liquid for relief. She was desiccating and decaying while still technically alive.

She had spent the last year of her life not remembering who anyone was, her few words being "Shut up!" or "Get out!," which she used profusely. They were accurate distillations of things she often meant to say before dementia but communicated less directly.

As the rest of the family were preparing for her death, I asked my mom to tell me more stories about Grandma.

"When you were a baby, if I left you with Grandma out in public to go pop into a store or something, when I came back, there you'd both be, surrounded by men."

"Was she flirty?" I asked my mom.

"She didn't even have to encourage them. That was the magic, she had some magnetic force. She was very easy to talk to," my mom said.

Her four daughters, me and my two brothers, the daughter of her already-dead brother, my grandfather (her ex-husband), his wife, and one of my other cousins all gathered at her care home the day we heard she had entered her final stage.

Her mouth was open and sunken around her toothless gums in a way that made my brother describe her as looking like a dementor from *Harry Potter*. The way she sucked in air, hard, like a bag was over her mouth, made her sound like one, too.

We sat with her for the entire day. We ate donuts from Tim Hortons in the TV room of the care facility and socialized like we weren't waiting for death. Some of my aunts stroked and squeezed her cheeks and kissed her forehead, calling on her to come out and say hi to the family.

"Everyone is here, Mom. Wake up!," they shouted, prodding her with affection she would have slapped them for if she had been... there.

When they decided to put her to bed, most of us went home.

Her daughters stayed with her, around the clock, twenty-four hours in rotations, for more than a week.

Before the death watch started, I had arranged a long-anticipated ski trip. I had never been close to my grandma and hadn't seen her in years, but if my mom needed me to be there for her, I would cancel the trip. "No, go," my mom urged. She had her sisters with her and there was nothing I could do but sit around waiting. I went to Calabogie with my friend Lana, it was only a handful of hours away, so I could race home if I was needed. My mom sent messages in a Facebook chat with me and my brothers titled "Grandma." Every day that update was the same. Still waiting. We were swinging in a liminal space, hanging on Grandma's every distressed breath.

When I got back, my brother Andrew drove me around town so I could run errands, and Ryan joined us for company. All of us felt useless and numb, and slightly – if shamefully – irritated.

When my mom was home, she would tell me about her childhood, the desperate lack of stability. Grandma and Grandpa divorced when my mom was thirteen. My mom and one of her sisters, being the two youngest, went to live with Grandma, and the two oldest daughters stayed with Grandpa.

Grandma could be bitter and manipulative, and life with her felt unstable. Precarious. She moved from job to job and town to town, setting tight restrictions on her daughters but failing to provide any sense of security. By the time my mom was fifteen, the stress of living with her mom had overwhelmed her so completely she was given tranquilizers to help her calm down. I had often protected my mom from Grandma's vindictive and judgmental attitude. But I had little idea of how terrible it had been for my mom as a young girl.

"When I had you, it was everything. You were finally my security and stability. The one thing that would always be with me," my mom told me. And I had left the second the opportunity presented itself, and then left again and again and again. My mom had always let me go easily enough, but she still seemed to think of me as her security, something stable in her life. During the most dramatically unstable times in my life, she had still leaned on me, not knowing how to recognize the signs of my distress. "I didn't know your divorce was so hard on you," she mentioned casually to me during one of our meandering debriefs on the state of Grandma and how it was making us think about our lives and the women that had influenced us. "I had no idea you were struggling then, you hid it so well!"

"Hid it?" I had heard my mom say this to me before, that I am so strong, that I hide my feelings. Although her words hurt and made me feel totally unstable, unsupported, and rejected, I'd always taken them at face value. It was probably true – I was overly guarded and that's why I couldn't get the support I needed. But in this case, I knew with certainty that I had been openly wrecked during my divorce. "Mom, people tell me all the time how clear my emotions read on my face..."

"Oh! I don't think it's you!" she said innocently, my entire lifetime of internalizing this dynamic rendered absurd. "I never notice these things. I'm not very observant. You have this trait you didn't get from me, or anyone else I know in this family," my mom explained. "It's pure you – you were just born intuitive. You can sense things about people and situations. You've always been very reflective. You were happiest when you could just play quietly in your room, reading or drawing and thinking to yourself. I never just sit around and think about things like you do." My mom still wanted to lean on me, to cast me as her source of stability. Maybe I had become a person who always leaves, as Elliott had named me, to escape and find stability for myself without that pressure.

Laura, whose mom died when she was young, gave me a message to pass on to my mom about Grandma: "All that bad stuff you inherited from her, or that happened with her, she's gathering it all up to take it with her where it can't hurt you anymore. If you want, let her. Let her take it all with her and leave you in the same peace she's headed for."

I do that with my dad. Whenever something reeks of abandonment daddy issues, I picture him in the dead-people place looking very helpful and I say, "You take that back! That is not mine, that's all yours. Take it back so I can make my life better than you left it." And he does.

I spent a lot of the holiday season rubbing knots out of my mom's neck and shoulders that she had gotten from sitting in hospital chairs at her mother's deathbed.

A week into waiting, the day before Grandma finally died, my aunt's husband was found dead from a heart attack. Their roommate called her while she was still at Grandma's deathbed.

"The 911 dispatcher told me to do CPR, but I couldn't even move him," their roommate reported, in complete shock.

"Grandma's at peace," my mom texted the group chat the next night. The words barely penetrated the fog of death in which we were lost.

I had just been with Misha eating poutine in a thick snowstorm, continuing our ongoing conversation based on an article about the "narrative fabric of the self" in mythical versus historical time. I was working out possible structures for the memoir I was going to Namibia to write, and she had been a wealth of inspirational sources.

My brother, picking us up from the restaurant and dropping Misha off at home, tilted his phone toward me so I could see the message. There was no emotional reaction from either of us. We did donuts, driving fast and then turning in tight circles trying to "spin out" on the slippery snow in his ancient Jeep Cherokee in an empty parking lot as the snow fell and fell and fell. Later, I would feel relieved for and supportive of my mom, and that was the entirety of my emotional reaction to the death of Grandma.

The next day, the rest of my cousins came in from out of town and gathered at my aunt's house for dinner. The door to my uncle's room where he'd died lay open and dark.

My grandmother had effortless charm, and I had been her infant apprentice. She also had flawless skin, movie star cheekbones, and a swift and impish sense of humour. Traits, I noticed as we gathered that night, she had passed on in unique and wonderful ways to all of the women who came after her.

Even in the midst of the incredible stress, there was this admirable calm. One cousin talked about how her dad's side of the family had been torn apart by petty arguments over a dead relative's will.

My aunt said, "I haven't even looked, I figured we'd do it after the funeral... we all basically know what there is and how it will be divided among us." No one remotely cared.

Family were gathering from across the province. Staggering arrivals meant catch-up conversations happened in intertwining loops. Two of my cousins started to talk about online dating. One who is now in a relationship reminisced about the unpleasant choice of men in her northern region of Ontario, joking mainly about the low-quality profile photos: their faces hardly visible under the proliferation of trucker hats, the ubiquity of shots featuring actual trucks. My other cousin, currently single, rued how it was even *worse* than that – men with *disabilities* were contacting her.

She was standing next to me and I was sitting on a barstool at eye height. "I think I'm pretty attractive," she said. "Why would a guy with an eye patch think I'd be into him?"

"I once had a short person message me, and I was like, buddy!," another cousin responded. She didn't even have to finish the sentence, the ridiculousness of his proposition spoke for itself.

"This is not my family," I thought to myself, retreating from the conversation into a familiar, detached quiet. I was in my hometown, surrounded by my family, but I was distinctly out of place. The room was full, but there was an emptiness for me. This was not where I felt known, or safe, or connected. I texted Laura, I scrolled through Instagram. When people asked me polite questions about being at the funeral, I answered with a polite regret: "I will be travelling and can't make it."

Hours later, the words would form: "If you think that about an eye patch, what do you think other people are thinking about a wheelchair?" Someone like me showing an interest in someone without a disability was still an insult to them. I thought of the kids in my seventh-grade class shouting: You like *Erin!*" Decades had passed, my adult cousins were essentially teasing each other the same way. And, just like seventh grade, I was sitting right there trying to pretend it had nothing to do with me.

When I mentioned to my mom what my cousins had said, she said, "You know, if someone tells a gay joke or a joke about mental health, I always say something like, hey, that's my son you're talking about. But my first thought when I heard your cousins was, well, they don't see you as disabled. That's a compliment! It didn't occur to me that when people make jokes about disabled people, they're talking about you."

It wasn't a compliment, but I think she understood that, so I said, "You know, it didn't occur to me either for the longest time, but I was so disconnected from myself, then. Now, I notice it because I work hard to keep those messages away from my heart and to defend other disabled people from them."

"Now I will notice it too," she promised.

The day after that, I flew out. I had already arranged the flights to get me from Toronto to Oranjemund, Namibia. Four flights, four days, a couple hotels, and a few meetings during layovers. It was too much to reschedule for a funeral when no one was sure when it would happen. So I missed it.

The day my grandma died, my mom told me every single detail of watching it happen. How Grandma would exhale and stop. Seconds would pass. They would lean in, ears to her chest and mouth, listening. And then Grandma would suck in another breath and they'd all sag back to their vigil spots.

Mom described Grandma's death down to the mottling of her skin as she quickly turned grey.

When my mom had spent the horror by telling it, she paused and tilted her head. "So, if I ever get to that state…"

"I'll take you out, don't worry," I said.

"Thanks," she sighed, relieved because she could believe me. The harsh way I sometimes love was good for something. Maybe this was the way in which she *did* have something that was finally hers, that she could always count on, that would always be there. All the people I loved could count on it. I leave, maybe, but I am still so present. No matter *where* I am, I am present. In my words, in my attention, I'm not just sitting alone in my room thinking about myself. I am thinking about *her*, about everyone I love, wanting to understand all the moving pieces so I can feel sturdy enough that I can give more love. And, because of all that time spent leaving and thinking, if the worst came to pass, I could be – I would be – present even through something as awful as a slow and ugly death.

"The hard part is knowing when," I mused. "What if you pass the point of being able to consent? How do I decide something like that?" I said.

"Now that I've seen it, I can tell you in advance, before my mind goes," she said in the same unaffected tone as most things she said.

"Lana wondered why someone didn't just smother Grandma," I said, reflecting her nonchalance because if I showed empathy, I knew it would make her cry and she hated to cry.

"I thought about it, actually," my mom said, again without any particular feeling. "There was a moment when I was alone with her and I thought about it." She paused for a minute, flicking through memories of all the things she learned about Alzheimer's over the years of Grandma's decline. And then, very matter-of-fact, as a point of interest, she continued, "They can tell when someone died from smothering. It shows somehow in the eyes."

CHAPTER TWENTY-SIX

Dispatches from the Desert, a Second Heart
Oranjemund, Namibia, January 2019

To get here, I had to beg the airport commissioner to let me on the tiny commuter plane headed to Oranjemund where I didn't know a soul. I am on a self-styled, solo writing retreat. All I have is a place to stay, and a task: Write a book – this book. To do the hard work, I have picked the perfect place. A place I know very little about. A place almost no one has visited. A place I only know about through a series of friendly synchronicities. I followed my curiosity. Curiosity feels like the proper state for writing a book.

My friend Sarah (with whom I hiked in the Himalayas) tried to send me a Valentine's Day present. "Give me your address when you're somewhere not Namibia," she texted. "DHL can't pinpoint the address you gave me."

"I feel very far away," I responded. I couldn't even give her a postal code, because the town does not have one. "Send it to Mary's house," I joked, but actually, yeah, that's kind of how it works.

"You ARE far. I looked up the town on a satellite map. I was, like, homegirl is in the middle of literal desert."

I hear jackals at night. Dogs in the neighbours' yards chatting with the jackals. Jackals have tails and noses like foxes, spots like deer, and the general air of puppies. They also have a very particular shuddering whine. I stay up all night with my words, and I hear these sounds: chirping crickets, a single moaning cat, barking dogs, howling jackals.

The first time I tried to imitate the jackals, I sounded like a horse. But jackals don't sound like horses. They make a high-pitched, very crisp "wheeeee" sound that burbles into an equally high-pitched neigh. Like they are very excited and keening at the same time. They sound like being very far away feels; space to go from one end of the emotional spectrum all the way to the other. To imitate a jackal, you can't hold back – there isn't a tame, indoor version. Fill your chest with air and wail.

Jackals. The desert. It sounds dramatic.

Yet I am tucked safely into the heart of a tiny, tranquil town with very friendly people and gardeners who water lawns or rake sand (it makes sense that landscaping in the desert would involve arranging sand) in front of tidy compounds without security bars or even locks. I am in the desert suburbs. At the *edge* of the literal desert, not in the middle of it, in a place hugging the Atlantic coast. A town that exists because of a diamond mine.

Diamonds are the town's genesis. Diamonds and a river. The town name means something like "the mouth of the Orange River." I think it's German in origin.

Oranjemund was founded, built, and owned by the mining company and was closed to the public until recently. Only employees and their families were permitted entry, they had to pass through a security checkpoint, and they were searched for diamonds each time they left. It was only in 2017 that the town was handed over to a public government and opened to outsiders.

Now, instead of security checkpoints, there is a boundary of trees planted around the entire perimeter of town. It blocks out most of the very intense wind that other coastal desert towns in Namibia have to put up with.

Oranjemund is transitioning. The mine is still here, but it has been threatening to close for the last ten years. The future of the town without the mine, open to an unfiltered public, is unfolding. Just as my future is unfolding.

What does it take to qualify as an oasis? Because I think I might be inside one. I would google it, but when I tried to look up "Oranjemund," the WiFi crashed. (In case you were wondering, the internet in a probable oasis can be inconsistent.)

The trees are thick and tall and shade every street. The eucalyptus and pine needles spend their scent in a trail as I crush them under my wheels. The flowers blaze color. Red hibiscus, white frangipani, bright pink flowers whose name I will never learn.

The wind makes the branches hum deeply, blowing cool and dry across the desert to bring me goosebumps. The town ends in a line of trees.

The other side of the treeline is vastness. Desert until the sea on one side. Desert until South Africa on another side. Desert until the rest of Namibia everywhere else. So much desert and distance. Undulating, unending space. Peace as far as the eye can see. The Spar, the grocery store where I go for my daily latte, also sells books on local history. On my first day in the town, I bought a memoir written about the Namibian struggle for independence.

In *To Hell and Back: My Experience Under Difficult Colonial Rule*, the author details the UN-supervised independence election. Dr. Tijiriange writes, "Namibia is, indeed, a product of international solidarity – more than any country that I know of."

Namibia is also, apparently, "the most arid country in the whole of southern Africa."

I thought it would be punishing, a desert climate, like it is in *The Little Prince* or *The Alchemist*. Instead, Oranjemund is mild. I am comfortable in my long-sleeved jean shirt, comfortable when I slip it off, comfortable when tongues of shadow lick the sunlight off my shoulder.

Every day, I discover a new mood of desert weather.

The house I live in is on one level. It is owned by a man I never met, who I was introduced to through a friend I had just met recently. When she heard through social media that her colleague was renting his house out in Namibia, she somehow thought of me. "The house is very remote and is part of a nature reserve or something," she said when she passed his contact on to me. We'd had only one (albeit in-depth) conversation previous to this and all she knew of this place was what she had read in the owner's brief post.

At the time she told me, I was thinking of this book and what I needed to write it. Space, tranquility, good weather, and the ineffable quality of serendipity that perfumes all my best experiences. Ineffable because I don't know if it's luck, or the natural result of the connections between people. I have let my life be so guided by the tingle of poetic coincidence that when I need something like a temporary homebase, and a colleague of an acquaintance of mine needs a temporary tenant, I think nothing of jumping at the chance. The risk of it doesn't occur to me. At least, not as a source of potential danger, I am following the thrill of fortuitous and unplannable events. Of course, I had never met the man whose house I would be occupying, and I was about to be alone in a foreign country, but when I reached out to my future host and told him I would like to stay in his house, he had a concrete ramp poured to the back door and told me if the locks were too high, he would send over a locksmith to lower them. Nothing is more welcoming than that.

My friend texts me to confess that, for a while, she was worried I wouldn't like Namibia, that her colleague and I wouldn't get along, or that I would have a terrible experience and it would be her fault, even that it might strain the professional relationship she had with her colleague. In reaching out to me and facilitating our connection, she had taken an impressive risk, too. My host was renting his home to a series of strangers while he was thousands of miles away. The sparkling and magical quality of my time here was made by an alchemy of intermingling risks.

When I need a break from writing, I explore town, wander by whim down streets I have not wandered before, taking note of the different trees, learning how the date palms grow with a squishy center, fresh fronds shooting up at the top and the ones underneath drying out, dying, breaking off. The stubs they leave form the tree's "trunk," but it is not wood. The core of the palm is like a pulpy heart inside a rib cage.

I am especially riveted by the town's edge. As edges often do, it comes abruptly. Neighbourhood… neighbourhood… nothing. My wheels are on the road, and after the edge of the road is sand, featureless until the horizon. I dip my wheels into the sand to make myself a part of the endless stretch of desert and see a herd of oryx, interspersed equidistantly between trees and perfectly camouflaged in the sand and shade. They take me in warily, chewing cud while in repose, exactly like unexotic cows.

Their dramatic markings make me tingle with appreciation. The way they're lined up, they look like a row of spectators to the soccer game happening on the other side of the treeline. I heard a story that the oryx horns, which are parallel, appear as a single horn when you look at them from the right angle, and that's the source of the unicorn myth. Across the road from the soccer-watching herd of oryx, I am the single figure in an empty vastness gazing across the road, perhaps across time, to the original unicorns.

Oranjemund is ten kilometres from the Atlantic coast. There are no boardwalks or beach loungers. It's not even suitable for everyday vehicles. My chair gets through. I push it backward like a four-wheeled wheelbarrow (big wheels leading the way). The sand is damp and salt-crusted, pebbled and warm. It makes a ringing sound when my wheels turn, swishing against the metal where it has gotten into my rims. The wheels are rusting and creaking from the dry and dusty weather, to which I then add this dampness. The waves crash, gallop, smash. And I sit quietly, trying to capture this majestic stretch of Namibian coast with my iPhone.

Later that day, I chat with a man sitting next to me in the café about writing and wheelchairing. While I sort through the hundred photos I have taken of the coast, I ask him if the coast has a special name I can tag the photos.

"The Skeleton Coast," he replies. "For all the wrecked ships along the shore."

"I thought that was further north," I say.

I google it. It's both. The actual skeletons – rusted hulls of sunken ships that have washed ashore – lie further north. The

Portuguese called the coast "The Gates of Hell," and the Namibian bushmen called it "The Land God Made in Anger."

"We just call it the coast," one of the waitresses chimes in, shrugging.

I feel a kinship with the wreckage, all the thrashing mighty water. What is a memoir, at least on some pages, if not a ship crashed and devoured to its skeleton by a mad sea, drowned to rust in the salty ocean depths, then spat out onto a desolate desert shore some god made in anger?

My neighbour is one of the managers of the Spar, where the Bean Tree café is located. The baristas ask me how my book is going and bring me lattes just the way I like them. One morning, my neighbour stops by my table buzzing with enthusiasm and introduces himself.

The news of me has spread through social circles, but it has gaps. I'm from Canada, they know that. But my neighbour has questions: What am I doing here? Do I know that of all the people to live in that house since the original owner – a man who had lived here for fifty years – I am the first to light the barbecue?

I tell the neighbour that I am a writer, I tell him that I am writing a book, I am writing everything that is happening right now, too. And in exchange he tells me that there are rivers, springs, secret places where, when it is not the time of a drought, you can crack the earth and water springs forth.

"Not a lot of people here know that," he says, indulging us both. He is a man who knows things not everyone knows, and I am a woman who would like to know them. I express my raw delight in the secrets of Oranjemund. And then he really grabs my interest when he says, "There are seven rivers under us."

I have been wondering about this before, but my unreliable desert WiFi has thwarted my research, so I let the fantasy simmer. Now I can confirm my dreams. Hesitantly, I begin, "If there are points of water that spring up naturally from under the ground..." my words pick up speed excitedly, my body leans in toward him, "doesn't that mean... this is... technically..."

He leans in, too, grinning, "...that Oranjemund is an oasis?," he finishes my words.

"Yes!" My eyes roll back in my head in pleasure. I have written my memoir in an actual desert oasis.

"Why don't people here know this?" I ask. I am curious why locals aren't equally delighted, why everyone isn't just falling all over themselves to declare, "We live in an oasis! Here is exactly how you can determine that! Let's go picnic at the places where the water breaks through the surface of the earth!"

"Well, historically, when the miners retired, they had to leave," he says.

"And the knowledge they had went with them," I conclude. He nods. Maybe the people who live *here* now know about the land, but I understand that Oranjemund was transient for most of its history. And lately, more and more generations are sent away to be schooled.

Another man pops into the café and exchanges a few words with my neighbour about the rain in the south. The sluices being open, the water would make its way here and raise the river.

"Did it rain here?" I ask, sad that I missed desert rain, though I had noted that the roads and sand – and even the air and sky – had been damp that morning. I had left my compound after waking and stood under the eucalyptus trees along the road just breathing.

"That," he scoffed, "was not rain. That was a deep mist. And it's what preserves life here.

When it rains, it's a whole different thing," he says. "The ground is hot and when the rain hits it, it steams and the smell is sweet and dry." He closes his eyes and sucks in a slow stream of air through his nose as if to savour the memory of that scent, giving me a chance to imagine how good it would be to smell it for myself.

My neighbour passes by my table regularly now, sliding into a seat between tasks. He asks how my writing is going. He has a WiFi extension installed in the café for me. The guy who runs the internet is also the three-time motocross champion of Namibia. My neighbour and the champion have an adventurous plan. Evidently the 4x4 club is going to drive up and down the massive piles of sand outside of town. Would I like to join?

The sand does not roll, it froths like tawny, streaming rivulets kicked up by the 4x4 tires and given to gravity. It flows under the tires like liquid. The first time I see it, I wonder where the water is coming from until my eyes adjust and I can see the grains of dry sand.

The wind makes the dunes, and the wind always changes. We are sliding, revving, rolling, and climbing across an inconstant landscape. In a month, these will be completely different dunes. In an hour, there won't even be a trace of our tracks.

There are no landmarks in a sand valley, no straight lines. There is sand for as far as the eye can see. How does anyone know where we are or how to get back? Someone says there's a trick to it, but they don't tell me the trick.

The sand blowing at the peaks betrays your eyes, you race to reach the top before knowing what is on the other side. There is barely a pause before a vertical plunge. Dewald is driving, and Nina (whose husband owns the vehicle) is in the back seat suffering the gravitational force where it is amplified as the Rover or Jeep or Isuzu picks up speed somewhere between racing down and racing back up the other side.

The peaks get higher and Nina jumps out of the vehicle. Dewald and I keep going. He pauses with the wheels of the 4x4 resting on either side of the tallest dune, to show me where the river pours through this plain of sand when it rains enough. For hours, Dewald drives, while I film, photograph, squeal. He drives me in a truck, and then I climb out the window so he can carry me to a quad bike, and he drives me up and down a dune on that. My arms wrap tight around his waist with fear, which evaporates when I feel his steady handling of the vehicle, so I press my hands against his back to hold myself upright so I can get a better view. Dewald looks for where my feet are, concerned with the combination of my lack of sensation and proximity to the scalding exhaust. He uses his foot to gently tuck each of mine back and out of the way as he drives the vertical side of the dune. I am so enthralled by landscape that I don't even notice until I see the video someone has taken of our run. Dewald gets us up and over and down the steepest, softest piles of sand I have ever seen. For a while, we are on another planet. But eventually we are tired of sand and want to go to the lake on Dewald's boat instead, so we leave.

We have only been twenty minutes outside of town the entire time.

While Dewald had been the driver, the truck actually belongs to Grant, a helicopter pilot for a company contracted to the mine. His wife, Nina, who had suffered the exaggerated g-force in the back seat during the dune racing, is a photojournalist and now runs a family law NGO.

When I use her toilet between dune race and river run, she hands me a book. Her memoir. She is a published author. I have come to the middle of nowhere, where I know no one, and managed to make friends with someone who has done what I am here to do: write a memoir. I take it as a solid omen. And since I like Grant and Nina's jovial, adventurous, welcoming vibe, I jump at the chance to join them when they invite me on a camping trip.

First, we drive through the blonde gravel plains of our home territory dotted with ostrich, then pass jagged black mountains with ridges like dinosaur backs and rubble piles. I find the natural formations so odd I keep asking what is mining leftovers and what is nature made.

We drive through more colours. Rosy mountains in the distance, wearing too much hot-pink blush for a daytime event. The horizon is a layer cake. Pink, then purple, then green – a ground covering of green stones, maybe lichens. I keep asking, "What rock is that?," every twenty kilometres. But there are too many landscapes, too much natural history to keep it all in my head.

"I need to lend you my geology book," Grant remarks.

From the backseat, Nina teases me that I'd come to Namibia an interesting person and would leave a person in love with... rocks.

We drive through more black mountains glistening with mica, some streaked with stripes of red sand from the Namib and more piles of rubble from abandoned mining sites. We are following the river, seeking a spot unlikely to flood during the night. The rains have fallen in the south and are on their way to the Orange River.

Grant and Nina set up an efficient camp. Bed rolls, serving-ware and cutlery, cool drinks, kebabs and corn over the fire for dinner.

"There's the poop stool!" Grant quite proudly plops a fold-able stool, covered in canvas with a hole in the centre on the ground by the truck. He bought it a while back when he was using a wheelchair to recover from a serious knee injury. "Burn your toilet paper, please. If you bury it, the wind will unbury it."

"A poop stool changes the whole game for me." Having something to sit on to toilet in the wilderness means I won't need any help. Of course what flashes through my mind is Mau helping me pee in the Andalucían mountains. That moment had built an intimacy I'd never felt with another person before, an intimacy that would lead to everything else.

I hadn't heard from him since arriving in Namibia almost two months before. Nothing when my grandma died, nothing about the issues I had with him asking to collaborate, nothing about the book I was writing and the feelings it brought up. "I am furious," I wrote in an email. Months ago, I had asked him to wait until I felt like contacting him. He almost instantly disregarded this instruction, emailing me about collaborating creatively, about a dream he had of me, about nothing in par-ticular. Basically I felt he was trying to pretend, and to force me to pretend, that nothing bad or good or intimate had ever happened. And then, the moment I relented, let him back in, he disappeared. How on earth do you love someone and not like them at the same time? When I had just arrived in Namibia, I was staring down the daunting adventure of the first page of a whole book. I wrote to him about how scared and emotional I was about that and how mad I still was at him. "If your strategy is to wait until the storm passes, then you should know I am still stormy." I meant for him to understand that it wasn't a storm that would pass while he half-watched, while he waited me out.

A month later, he texted to say he was completely exhausted from work. Someone (the same guy as before?) had broken up with him again, he was stressed out when he thought of sitting down to write me, he was sorry. "Oh look, there I've gone and disappeared again." It was not an apology, it was not even a real acknowledgment of how his actions affected me. Then he wrote, "How have things been for you?"

I ignored it and went camping.

Here, there is another text, "How have things been?"

"Things are good. But I don't want to catch up with you on everything." I text a photo of me at the camp site. A throwback to when I would send him twenty or thirty selfies and an hour's worth of reading of my stories to catch up. Now my messages are as mixed as his. In truth, I *desperately* want to catch up on everything. I *want* him to tell me how gorgeous I look and tell me everything about his life. But I know it isn't good for me to try to keep up this intimacy. He hasn't even mentioned the updates I'd already given him.

"The stress of you disappearing and appearing randomly was getting bad. This month has been a good break for me. I'm happy and at peace. I'd like to keep things this way between us," I type, taking a moment to brace myself with the courage to say it.

"It makes me super happy to hear this has been a good break and that you are happy and at peace," he types back. "There is nothing more important than that. I love you so much. How much longer are you in Namibia?"

Wait? *Now* he says he loves me? And he's happy I don't want to be in contact? Maybe he misunderstands.

"Mau, I meant the break between us," I clarify. "I liked not being in contact. I want that to continue." My heart races from saying this kind of goodbye. I want to hold on, I need to let go. I am barely sure of myself. Clarity in my mind and heart flashes as brief as lightning, as embers, as fireflies, then are smothered by the darkness of my uncertainty and grief. How on earth do those bugs follow the light to each other so effectively?

"That's what I mean, too. And if that's what you prefer, that's what we'll do. Apologies in advance for random messages that I may want to send to say hello," he writes back.

Defiance isn't typically a romantic quality. It isn't generally characterized as sensual or harmonious or any of the things that relationships and hearts are noted for being drawn to or needing. But it had been what I needed throughout my life, and I was sensual and romantic. It had given me my dignity when that was the only thing I could command from my circumstances. When faced with insurmountable obstacles, defiance made me brave and clear and it had a way of making the total uncertainty and steady risk of failure fun. There is a seductive rush to defiance. It needed heart and focus to keep it honest and fuelled. But defiance was what made me. All this time I had been trying to claim a space for myself in romance. I wanted a love that could go all the way, but first I had to include myself in the choreography of romance – hard to do on my own. Then Mau came along and we conquered a parcel of the romantic landscape for ourselves. But sometimes what you defy aren't just the limits people impose on you; you also have to defy the limits you yourself internalized. I still saw love for myself. But what did it mean to me that after all we'd shared, Mau was opting out?

I was still defiant. But now Mau and I weren't defying the odds together, he was defying me, my heart.

"If you know to apologize for it, then why do it? Please don't send me random messages! You have said before that you would lay low, follow my lead, give me space, only to pop back in a week later with 'random hellos.' You're not listening," I text, resolved sadness washes through me and mixes with the pure nature I am soaked in, which throbs throughout my body.

"Copied." Thumbs up. Emoji with a zippered mouth. "Let me know if/when you want to hear from me again," he texts, and I relax. Not because I am at peace with him or with us, but because I have stopped fighting myself. I am at peace with me.

"That whole affair would never have happened if I had had a poop stool," I say to Grant and Nina at the campsite.

Grant pops a champagne cork, and we toast to our whole affair instead.

A toast to Nina freshly moved to Oranjemund, a toast to the beauty of Namibia, a toast to an adventurous life all the way lived, a toast to new friends. We toast to the owl hooting interjections as we talk the sun down. Fireflies streak the night above our heads, flying close enough to the fire to imitate embers.

The full moon rises from behind our mountain view as the sun sets, washing the moon, the sky, and the mountain in a pink glow. The fire crackles.

"When there's no moon, the stars are so bright you can't make out the constellations. The moon is so bright, you can see colour at night," Grant says.

I sleep with moonlight on my face, the sound of wild animals stomping the soft ground in irritation that we are sleeping in their path around the river. I wake to the glow of sunrise, coffee on the fire, Grant surveying the campsite for the tracks of the animals that encountered us in the night. "Desert zebra, a wild cat, mongoose maybe," we muse. "Possibly a baboon over here?"

Before the sun can rise too high and hot at the campsite, we clean up every trace of ourselves and drive off in search of swimming holes.

We drive across the riverbed of the Fish River Canyon. Find leopard tracks. The print of a giant heron. Leave our own tracks. Then we pull up at the edge of water, where the sand is baked to a crust.

I menstruate freely in the water in a pair of red underwear. I swim topless. And by swim, I mean I crawl through the bath-warm water on my hands and knees so my hands can feel for underwater rocks and protect my feet. My nipples brush against the water that ripples sensuously from my movements, the tips of my hair soaking like the tendril branches of a willow tree. I water-crawl to a half-submerged rock, pull myself up on it to sun myself like a river mermaid. I request a photo shoot.

I am travelling with a former firefighter-turned-helicopter-pilot, with years of actual danger-honed rescue skills, and with a renowned South African photojournalist. We pool our skill sets and scheme an outdoor art project.

From my rock perch, I specify that I'd love to do the photo shoot with my wheelchair. Grant is happy to haul my chair across the river to me while Nina uses my wide-angle iPhone lens to document our adventure.

And again, as we drive out, we pause for another shoot. We have to tread carefully across the sand, heated by the midday sun, as it is much too hot to touch with bare skin. Grant hoists my chair, then me, on top of the tallest rock in the middle of the dry riverbed. I have to be careful to only touch my wheelchair, to avoid the skin-scalding rock. He crouches behind the rock to get out of the shot, his butt stuck up in the air, while Nina focuses the texture of the sand in the foreground and then adjusts to focus the vastness of the canyon, and adjusts again to get the curve of the rocks leading up to me, the centrepiece, the sex icon, the living and momentary monument.

The river is as inconstant as the dunes we had raced across days earlier. The water level sinks and rises with the rains. It can flood in the span of half an hour, washing out roads and bridges and unprepared people. It dries out, leaving fish stuck in the gravelbed, on which happy otters feast.

When you want to swim, you have many assessments to make. You know the places you've swam before; you check the progress the river has made and the water reports; you calculate; you run contingencies in your mind constantly – how would we get back to the road if we broke down here, etc.

There is no site that has been prepared for people, nature does what it will do, and we encounter it, test it for safety and welcome, earn our place within it.

We marvel at and appreciate the chance to be here, our bodies cooling in the freshwater, our laughter ricochets off the mountainside.

Nature isn't sentimental about me. If I crawl to get through a forest trail, nose close to the dirt, or take double the amount of time to hike the same distance as my able-bodied friends, nature isn't inspired by me. It doesn't pity me or admire me. It isn't any more resistant to me than it is to anyone else. Nature lets me take my risks, find or make my place, it opens itself completely. The entire breadth of nature's heart – as generous in its nourishment as it is in its cruelty – is open to me.

My flesh is of the earth, like all bodies. But so is the body of my wheelchair, the titanium extracted from the crust of the earth, an element that happens to be abundantly found in Canada. The same crust of ancient rock I crawled across as a kid contains the element, the oxide, needed to build my wheelchair. Titanium is always bonded to other elements in nature.

Titanium is paramagnetic. When it is exposed to a strong magnetic force, it internalizes that magnetism, forming its own magnetic field in response to the magnetic field around it. This sounds to me exactly like the mechanics of love, of adventure, of a magical life. Expose yourself to a greater force, internalize it until it forms within you a resonating force, then radiate outward. It's a *seduction*.

The titanium of my wheelchair is alloyed, bonded to, made solid with aluminum. It is known in this state for having the lowest density with the highest strength of all the metals, for being able to resist the damaging effects of extreme environments, for being lustrous. The same metal used for spacecraft and jets is used to make my wheelchair. It was made to explore. Titanium was named for the sons of Gaia, the primordial mother of all life on Earth. When I roam, when I roll, when I fly, I am held up by the spirit of titans.

After Grant, Nina, and I finish swimming, we take ourselves for ice cream. "Something with caramel, please," I request, and Grant brings me a Rolo ice cream bar.

Then it is the long lull of the drive home, back through the pink mountains, the tiger-striped mountains, the black dinosaur mountains, the quiver trees with bone-white trunks and leafless branch stumps gilded in gold, and the blonde sand, red sand, horizon upon horizon upon horizon.

My eyes are open, but my brain is asleep. Grant and I sing old country songs to each other, and Nina falls into actual sleep in the backseat.

In the late afternoon, I crawl into my bed inside a house inside a town, inside a desert oasis, the wild still throbbing through me.

I sleep with the sun beating inside my skin, a whole-body pulse, a second heart.

CPSIA information can be obtained
at www.ICGtesting.com
Printed in the USA
LVHW091626250820
664208LV00002B/350

9 788792 633552